M000074513

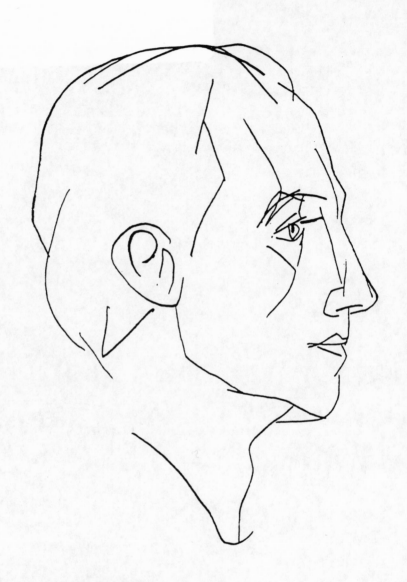

pour Dominique Eluard
picasso

Paul Eluard

OMBRES ET SOLEIL
SHADOWS AND SUN

Selected Writings
of 1913 - 1952

Translations by Lloyd Alexander and Cicely Buckley

Illustrations by A. Lhote, Chagall, Picasso, Magritte

OYSTER RIVER PRESS

Permission for the use of writings by Paul Eluard has been granted by Les Editions Gallimard, editors of his *Oeuvres complètes* (Bibliothèque de la Pléiade); by Les Editions de Minuit for poems from *Poésie et vérité* and *Au rendez-vous allemand*; by Les Editions Seghers for poems from *Le dur désir de durer, Le temps déborde* and *Le phénix*.

Translations by Lloyd Alexander, in *Paul Eluard: Selected Writings* (Eds. Gallimard, 1951) reprinted as *Paul Eluard: Uninterrupted poetry: selected writings* (New Directions 1975), are reprinted by permission of New Directions Publishing Corp. All rights reserved. "You rise the water unfolds"; "Patience"; "Stopping the hours"; "Curfew"; "From the outside"; "Critique of poetry"; "On the human scale"; "In Spain".

Illustrations from lithographs, drawings & etchings by André Lhote, Marc Chagall, René Magritte and Pablo Picasso are reproduced with permission of the Musée d'Art et d'Histoire de Saint Denis, France, and the Houghton Library at Harvard University.

The cover design is from an etching by Pablo Picasso for Eluard's book *La Barre d'appui*, 1936.

OYSTER RIVER PRESS
20 Riverview Road Durham, New Hampshire 03824-3313 USA

ACKNOWLEDGEMENT

La poésie doit être faite par tous, non par un.
(Poetry must be made by all, not by one alone.)

Lautréamont

In keeping with this principle which guided the Surrealist writers and painters, I have benefited from the interest of good friends and mentors. The poet's daughter Cécile Eluard, and his wife Dominique Eluard, encouraged me to complete translations for this selection of his writings. Lucien Scheler, his long-time friend and co-editor of the collection of Paul Eluard's *Oeuvres complètes*, first published in 1968, gave me good counsel.

Lloyd Alexander, translator for Eluard's *Selected Writings* (Editions Gallimard, 1951), republished in 1975 as *Paul Eluard: Uninterrupted Poetry* by New Directions, has contributed a number of his translations unchanged, as listed on the page of permissions.

Professor David Lenson at the University of Massachusetts (Amherst) gave constructive criticism and direction as I undertook the translations. Thanks also to Professors Mimi Carre, Don Levine, Richard Tedeschi, Anne Hyde Greet, and to the memory of Micheline Dufau, who inspired so many students.

Hélène Cantarella, Professor Emerita of French and Italian, was Chief of the Foreign Language Section of the Motion Picture Bureau of the American Office of War Information in World War II; as a translator and editor, she made important suggestions for interpreting Eluard's language. Others have shared valuable insights: Stuart M. Leiderman, Ed Carpenter, Maggie Bogle, Robert G. Hoddeson, Nacera Belaidi, Béatrice Pépier, Tara Welinsky and Walter Buckley.

C. B.

CONTENTS

III. THE TIME OF THE RESISTANCE 1940-1944

IV. THE TIME OF RESOLUTION 1945-1952

ix

ILLUSTRATIONS

LOOKING AT THE TWENTIETH CENTURY [1]

*I can't help thinking that this has been the most violent century in
human history.*

William Golding, Nobel Laureate, writer

*I would say that it raised the greatest hopes ever conceived
by humanity, and destroyed all illusions and ideals.*

Yehudi Menuhin, musician

*In spite of everything there have been revolutions for the better
in this century...the rise of the fourth estate, and the emergence
of women after centuries of repression.*

Rita Levi Montalcini, Nobel Laureate, scientist

What Eric Hobsbawm calls The Age of Catastrophe lasted from 1914
to the aftermath of the Second World War. The first "Great War" of
1914-1918 for him marked the breakdown of western civilization of the
nineteenth century. The Twentieth Century has been deeply scarred by
two world wars, two waves of global rebellion and revolution, the
crumbling of huge colonial empires and a modern industrial colossus,
world economic crises that brought even the strongest economies to their
knees, and is concluding with a continuous series of smaller but deadly
conflagrations, rebellions and terrorist attacks.

Paul Eluard has recorded the events he witnessed in this Age of
Catastrophe, so that those who follow will learn from the past, to insure
a just world for future generations.

---

[1]Quotations in Eric Hobsbawm, *The Age of Extremes* (N.Y: Pantheon, 1994).

La poésie doit avoir pour but la vérité pratique.

Poetry must have as its goal practical truth.

Louis Aragon, Preface to *Poèmes politiques*

Selected poems and essays by Paul Eluard are presented here from twenty-eight of his books. These reflect his love and loss; they record his friendships among artists and writers searching for an adequate response to the cataclysmic events of the first half of the twentieth century. Eluard played a crucial role in raising awareness of the need for durable solutions as his poems were translated into many languages.

His poems cover four periods: his early years through World War I, between the two World Wars, the French Resistance during the German Occupation of World War II, and after the Liberation of France in 1944. The brief history that follows records the circumstances that brought about an important evolution in a poet's outlook and in the language he used to communicate his ideas.

Paul Eluard . . .

Born in 1895, Eugène Emile Paul Grindel (who later took his maternal grandmother's surname, Eluard) grew up in the working-class suburb of Saint Denis. He moved to Paris with his family in 1908. His studies were interrupted in 1912-1913 while he recuperated from a lung ailment at a sanitarium in Davos, Switzerland. There he read widely, including works of the contemporary avant-garde poets, Max Jacob and Apollinaire, who were exploding the traditional literary conventions of subject, meter and rhyme in poetry. He was moved by Walt Whitman's compassion for the wounded and dying soldiers of the American Civil War, and his celebration of democracy and the common man, in the recently translated *Leaves of Grass*. At Davos, Eluard met the Russian-born "Gala." His health restored, he returned to Paris in February, 1914. Following the outbreak of the "Great War" in which almost an entire generation of Frenchmen would lose their lives, Eluard was mobilized in December into the French Army, assigned as medic to the twenty-second section of military nursing. Horrified at the suffering of thousands evacuated to his hospital after the autumn offensive of 1916, he requested a transfer back to the infantry. The following February, while on a three-day leave from military duty at the front lines, he and

1

Gala were married. After being hospitalized twice with acute bronchitis in that year, he served only in the auxiliary, returning to Paris to his wife and newborn daughter, Cécile, in 1918.

The publication of his first books, *Le devoir et l'inquiétude* (*Duty and misgivings*, 1917) and *Poèmes pour la paix* (*Poems for Peace*, 1918) brought recognition and an introduction to other writers, Louis Aragon, André Breton and Philippe Soupault, who produced the first issue of *Littérature*, beginning an unusually creative period for artists and writers intent on exposing and overcoming the causes of war and corruption.

The Surrealists, breakers of chains . . .

Eluard and his new friends joined the Dadaist movement, a call-to-arms "against the agony of the times and against inebriation with death," led by the Roumanian writer, Tristan Tzara.[1] With new insight into the psyche and pathologies of erratic behavior, they attacked the "inconsistency and inanity" of romanticism as responsible for "clouding the eyes" of the "superpatriots" and perpetrators of war. Many considered the Dadaists to be subversives intent on disrupting the conventions of established society.

Dissatisfied with the limitations of the solely destructive criticism of Dada, Breton, Aragon, Eluard and others broke away to regroup in the pursuit of "surrealist" or "superrationalist" goals, hoping to achieve greater understanding of human nature and human need. They decided to explore a world of unfettered joys and fears, of love and laughter, a realm akin to the timeless, fantasmagoric place of *La bonté, contrée énorme où tout se taît* (*Kindness, the huge domain where all is hushed*) as Apollinaire had suggested in his poem "La jolie Rousse" (*Calligrammes*, 1918). They would invent "a new language," as Rimbaud had proposed five decades earlier: *Que les choses parlent (Let things speak for themselves).*

The Surrealists experimented with memory and the revelations of dreams through automatic writing, hypnotic trance and free association. After conducting initial séances where mind-altering substances were used to enhance the imagination, they turned to self-hypnosis and the

---

[1] Hugo Ball, *Diary of June 18, 1916.* Cited in William S. Rubin, *Dada and Surrealist Art*, (NY: Harry Abrams, 1968), 16.

invocation of "pure" imagination. In the first issue of *La Révolution Surréaliste* of 1924 they announced that Surrealism was at the crossroads of the forces of enchantment:

> *Surrealism opens the door of the dream to all those for whom night hungers. Surrealism is at the crossroads of the enchantments of sleep, of alcohol, tobacco, ether, opium, cocaine, morphine; but it is also the breaker of chains, we sleep no more, we don't drink, we don't imprison, we don't inject ourselves but we dream, and the rapidity of the needles of lamps introduces into our brains the marvelous deflowered golden sponge.*

> (Signed by) J.-A. Boiffard, P. Eluard, R. Vitrac

In the Surrealist Manifesto of the same year, Breton claimed that poetry would lead the way to truth through the expression of "automatic revelations," in the absence of all control by the faculty of reason, or by esthetic and moral preoccupations. A surrealist *event* was a discovery of the imagination revealing an unspoken unity between inner consciousness and outward appearances, between the inner man and the public figure. In the *Déclaration of January 27, 1925*, the Surrealists stated their intention to record "revolutionary altruism" in honest demonstration: *Surrealism is not a new or easier means of expression....it is a means of total liberation of the mind....Rather than attempt to change conventional morality, we intend to demonstrate the fragility of such thinking.*

"'Change the world,' said Marx; 'Change life,' said Rimbaud. These propositions, for us, are one and the same," claimed Breton.[1]

. . . and his friends the painters

Eluard's friends the painters (visionary brothers, seers, *les frères voyants*) illustrated many of his books, inspired by his imagery, imbued with sunlight to expresses the joy in love, in the life of the couple and

---

[1]*André Breton, Entretiens avec A. Parinaud* (Gallimard, 1952) 105-6; cited in *Paul Eluard: Oeuvres Complètes II*, 1388. Few of the Surrealists relinquished their independence as artists; yet they were inspired by Marx's ideal of humanizing the lives of working people, and with many others they saw the Russian Revolution of 1917 as a movement of liberation.

the family, while his metaphors of night and shadows evoke death and solitude. His human frailty increased his intense appreciation of life in all its manifestations. In *The animals and their men, men and their animals* (1921), illustrated by André Lhote, the reliable instinct and simple dignity of the lonely old horse, the cat and the fish, are apparent, as they maneuver for survival, as does the man. The animals, "the useless ones," are compared to man working in "order and disorder." In "Dampened," none can resist death by work or by reasoning. *The water, like a skin none can wound, Is caressed by man and by fish. Snapping like a bowstring, The fish, when caught by the man, Expires....But man sinks to the waters' depths For the fish, or for the bitter solitude Of supple, unyielding waters.*

Eluard prepared commentaries that were published alongside his friends' drawings. He worked with the German artist Max Ernst, who lived for a while with Eluard and Gala, in the production of *Au Défaut du silence* (*For lack of silence,* 1925). He also provided the words to "illustrate" Man Ray's dreamlike drawings for *Les mains libres* (*Free hands,* 1937).

Eluard's best Surrealist verbal collages are reminiscent of Chagall's magical use of metaphor, freeing the laws of gravity, as in his painting of the young lover who floats across a room to bestow a kiss upon his beloved; and where donkeys and violinists, floating in the night sky, serenade villagers below. In Eluard's poem "L'amoureuse" (1924) the beloved is the reflection of her lover: *She is standing on my eyelids And her hair is mingled with mine, She takes on the color of my eyes, Is lost in my shadow like a stone against the sky.*

The expression of love is a catalyst for seeing more clearly, more intuitively, in *L'amour la poésie* of 1929, Part V: *Plus c'était un baiser/ Moins les mains sur les yeux* (*The more complete the kiss/the clearer our vision*). Without any logical relationship, sensual, erotic images are juxtaposed (a technique adopted by modern advertising for its power of subjective persuasion). Readers may associate freely to find the connections behind the appearances of unrelated objects juxtaposed. In *Love~poetry* (1929) *the earth is a blue orange, and wasps flower green.* Drawn into a fantasy world, we engage in a game of looking and sensing reality. A blue orange may suggest the earth in shadow at night, or the after-image of the sun, imprinted on the eye of the beholder in its complementary color. "Poetic objectivity exists only in the succession, in the linking of all the subjective elements of which the poet is...not the master, but the slave" *(La Rose publique,* 1934).

. . . the changing image of woman . . .

Lucien Scheler (in his preface to *Paul Eluard: Oeuvres Complètes*) describes the poet as "a prey to contradictions" when he left Marseilles for the Orient in March, 1924, on a "liberating" trip around the world, wanting to "erase everything," leaving a note only for his father. The next day his *Mourir de ne pas mourir (To die from not dying)* appeared; "this last book" was dedicated to André Breton "to simplify everything." Gala and Max Ernst came to meet him a week later; he returned from his voyage in October. Breaking the silence, subsequent poems express his continued fascination for Gala, for the mystery of love that "creates and frees" him, the pain he experienced from "having or not having....the one who denies absence" and who gives him life. ("Celle de toujours, toute," *Capitale de la douleur/* "One forever, everything," *Capital of sorrow*, 1926).

When they separated again in 1930, Gala went to live with Salvador Dali in Spain. Eluard came out of his despondency when he met and eventually married a delicate woman of Czech parentage, Nusch, who helped him to recognize his responsibility to all men, and who was his constant companion until her untimely death in 1946:

Laissez-moi donc juger de ce qui m'aide à vivre....Après le plus grand abandon....Vivre c'est partager je hais la solitude....Le seul abri possible c'est le monde entier....Vivre se perdre afin de retrouver les hommes....

(*Let me judge what helps me to live....After the greatest abandon....Living is sharing, I hate solitude....the only safe haven is the entire world....Living is to lose oneself in order to find others again...*)

"Portrait," *Poèmes Politiques*, 1948

. . . from the horizon of one to the horizon of all . . .

While true poetry belongs to the realm of the imagination, circumstances require that we speak out against complacency and for freedom in this "banal, vulgar, impossible world that misfortune constantly breaks down." Poetry is "as much a part of the cold necessity, of knowing and eating better, as of the taste for the marvelous." So said Eluard at the first International Exhibit of Surrealist Art in London in 1936, encouraging writers to support movements of liberation, while volunteers from many countries were joining the International Brigade in Spain to support the "Republicans" who had been ousted from government by more conservative forces.

The Nazi bombing of a Basque city in broad daylight, on market day, so shocked Picasso that he began the drawings for his famous painting "Guernica," while Eluard wrote to inform the world of the tragedy where over 2,000 civilians were killed. When Madrid was under siege, Eluard urged people to care for their "sensitive" cities and life-giving oceans, forests and plains, even as they cast off their chains *(En Espagne*, 1937). Speaking from his own experience, the poet held out the promise that humans weary of living in the "ruins of sleep," of "fatigue and abandon," will rise to overcome their lethargy ("Sans âge," *Cours naturel*, 1938) in order to improve living for all of humanity.

In 1939 the Republican Partisans in Spain could no longer resist the superior Fascist forces. The Nazi invasion of Eastern Europe was followed by the defeat of Western European countries in 1939, and the bombing of London. The United States entered the war in 1941.

At the German Rendezvous: The French Resistance

Demobilized after Maréchal Pétain surrendered the French troops in June, 1940, Eluard chose to remain in France during the German Occupation to work with the French Resistance movement. He dreamed of freedom for "the innocents, a multitude at last united" *(Sur les pentes inférieures / On the lower slopes*, 1941). He organized writers still remaining in France into the "Comité national des écrivains" in support of the Resistance of the northern zone of France; Aragon led the writers of the south. They often wrote poems on cigarette papers to be swallowed if they were searched by the Gestapo. When his *Poetry and Truth* (1942) was denounced by the German Institute as a dangerous tract, Eluard went into hiding, moving frequently to avoid arrest. His poem "Liberté," parachuted by the RAF over occupied France, was translated into many languages and circulated among the Allied troops in North Africa preparing for the invasion of Europe.

Notices of terrorist reprisals posted daily by the Germans were one source of Eluard's poignant "poems of circumstance" circulated among the *Maquis* (Resistance units), published in 1944 as *Les Armes de la Douleur (The Arms of Sorrow)*, appearing again in *Au rendez-vous Allemand (At the German rendezvous)* later the same year.

6

Voir, c'est comprendre, juger, transformer, imaginer,
oublier ou s'oublier, être ou disparaître.

Donner à voir, 1939 [1]

As early as 1920 Eluard had defined a basic goal for his writing as the expression of "the beauty that is truth," as opposed to romantic concepts of beauty rooted in the "sentimental exaltation" of several literary epochs. He broke away from presenting a logical story in "gently rocking," rhymed verse, preferring the tone of familiar conversation, direct language which can help others see the joys and the misery, show the poverty of human lives. Picasso echoed his concern:

What do you think an artist is? An imbecile who has only eyes if he's a painter, ears if a musician, or a lyre at all the levels of the heart if a poet, or only muscles if he's a boxer? On the contrary, he is at the same time a political being, constantly on the alert before the destructive, burning or quiet events of the world, making himself adapt to their image.

How is it possible not to be interested in other people, and by virtue of what ivory tower of nonchalance, to become detached from a life brought to us so copiously? No; painting is not made to decorate apartments. It is an instrument of offensive and defensive war against the enemy. [2]

Such a gift for seeing can bring people together. *Voir, c'est comprendre et c'est agir: c'est unir le monde à l'homme et l'homme à l'homme.*

(Seeing is understanding and taking action, uniting the world to man, and man to man.) Preface to *Anthologie sur l'Art* (1952-1954)

---

[1] Seeing is understanding, judging, transforming, imagining, forgetting or forgetting oneself, being or disappearing. *Helping others to see*, 1939.

[2] Eluard quoted Picasso in "L'amour en guerre," a radio broadcast of 1946, reproduced in *Europe*, 642 (Oct. 1982), 160-165.

Poésie engagée or "committed poetry"

Eluard's poems of the thirties and forties recall a shared history. In "Courage" of 1944, Paris is seen as a resourceful old woman, cold and hungry; despite her pallor and her ill-fitting clothes, there is courage in her eyes. Addressed in the familiar "tu" (thou), she symbolizes the whole population waiting for liberation:

Ne crie pas au secours Paris....Tout ce qui est humain se révèle en tes yeux / Paris ma belle ville/Fine comme une aiguille forte comme une épée / Ingénue et savante / Tu ne supporte pas l'injustice

(Don't cry for help Paris....All that is human is revealed in your eyes / Paris my beautiful city / Fine as a needle strong as a sword / Simple and knowing / You do not support injustice)

In *Uninterrupted Poetry* (1946) the poet's voice (*Are there two of us or am I alone/ Like a solitary woman?*) alternates with the voice of a woman. A torrent of adjectives describes her many facets: *naked, wiped out, sleepy, chosen, sublime, solitary...global, haughty, popular...impardonable, black, humiliated, exploded!* She sees her life repeated in the lives of her time-weathered mother and her fair-skinned child. This shared history with its half-serious word play contrasts the woman with the man, caught up in his *slow barbarism, confused instinct, his eyes closed like a swamp, his flesh in exile, always isolated, undone.* Yet he is *responsible, mortal, divided, his brow bleeding with hope.* Together, man and woman live to be faithful to life itself:

Nous deux toi toute nue
Moi tel que j'ai vécu
Toi la source du sang
Et moi les mains ouvertes
Comme des yeux

Nous deux nous ne vivons que pour être fidèles
À la vie

(We two and you naked / Myself just as I have lived
You the fountainhead of blood / I with my hands open/Like eyes
We two live only to be faithful / To life.

Poésie ininterrompue, 1946)

. . . .

8

In his preface to Eluard's *Political Poems* of 1948, Aragon asked that we read them like a newspaper "for the news of a world to come." He proclaims the end of the "incredible opera" of romantic poetry for "life has caught up with the fable;" words must mean what they say, and "poetry must have practical truth as its goal." Aragon speaks of his friend's use of "honest language" to describe the "heaven and hell" of life on earth. Eluard's voice is that of "a lone man in a deserted palace adorned with high mirrors....whose voice is the conscience of a world of stones and echoes, a man who sees beyond the walls the hidden significance of things and who speaks, in the midst of the dumb and deaf, the very language of the future," a future imbued with golden light, changing seasons, and seeds bursting in springtime, the reflection of human lives regenerated.[1] Even though his health was failing, the poems of *The Phoenix* (1951) convey this sense of renewal, inspired by Dominique, whom he met at a World Peace Convention in Mexico.

> *I love you . . . .*
> *For the smell of the open air and the smell of warm bread*
> *For the snow that melts for the first flowers*
> *. . . .*
> *I love you for your wisdom that is not mine*
> *For well-being*
> *I love you against all that is only illusion*
> *For this immortal heart I do not detain*
> *You think you are doubt and you are only reason*
> *You are the great sun that goes to my head*
> *When I am sure of myself.*

Here he uses *reason* in its positive meaning as the sum total of awareness, requiring that we take control of our own destiny. We must ask the questions before we are questioned. Freedom is the foundation on which society must be rebuilt, with the strength of redeeming love.

To express these goals in *Pouvoir tout dire* (*To be able to tell it all*, 1951) Eluard returned to the twelve-syllable alexandrines, alternating with shorter eight and ten syllable verses of early Provençal and Catalan ballads. Like poems of the oral tradition, these verses appeal to the memory of recently shared history. It is the poet's responsibility to make

---

[1] Louis Aragon, Preface to "Uninterrupted Poetry" in *Paul Eluard: Selected Writings*. L. Alexander, translator, 1951.

us aware of the events, so that we may learn from the past, in order to take a long view and act for future generations:

> *Comprenez-moi je veux vous donner à penser*
> *Que tout n'a pas été si facile ni gai*
> . . . .
> *Hommes de l'avenir il vous faut voir hier*
> *Je vous parle des morts qui sont morts sans printemps*

"Le grand souci des hommes de mon temps" (1951)

> *(Understand me I want to give you food for thought*
> *How everything has not been easy nor fun*
> . . . .
> *Men of the future you must see yesterday*
> *I speak of the dead who died without a springtime*

"The great worry of the men of my time")

Cicely Buckley
Durham, NH
March 21, 1995

10

On translations

Eluard's use of basic, common language is a challenge for the translator. A "re-creation" in English is most often achieved with a close translation. A metaphor such as "le front pur," denoting a fresh outlook, uncorrupted by habits of language or of ideas, can only be translated as the poet's "pure brow." The meaning is seldom the same for distinct cultures; *bread* in English, *Brot* in German and *pain* in French bear different connotations. And while chrysanthemums may suggest colorful autumn to a New Englander, most French will associate them with a pilgrimage to the cemetery on All Soul's Day. "Man" or "people" may translate "homme" and "les hommes" used in the generic sense as "humankind." "C'est un homme" ("he's a real man") in many countries still implies that a man is especially trustworthy and courageous.

When a quite literal translation was misleading, we looked for an alternative to convey the poet's intended meaning. Often we arrived separately at the same solution. It is not important to attribute the translations to one or the other (except those listed on the page of permissions). We expect that each poem will be created anew according to the experience of each reader or interpreter.

The present selection complements translations undertaken by Lloyd Alexander after World War II with the guidance of the poet himself, reprinted in 1975 as *Uninterrupted poetry* with testimonials by Aragon, Louis Parrot and Claude Roy. Several pieces not previously available in English, to our knowledge, are from *Les animaux et leurs hommes les hommes et leurs animaux* (1920), *Les nécessités de la vie et les conséquences des rêves* (1921), and *Pouvoir tout dire* (1951).

In Part V, prose writings (here in English only) include the Surrealists' Declaration of 1925, pieces on the nature of "committed poetry"—*poésie engagée*—and on the "unintentional poetry" created by all of us as we speak of our daily lives. Eluard speaks of the responsibilities of the poets in *The future of poetry*. Two essays complement his eulogy to Picasso in his book *Donner à voir*.   C. B.

I

1913 - 1919

POEMES de JEUNESSE

POEMS of YOUTH

LE FOU PARLE

C'est ma mère, monsieur, avec ma fiancée.
Elles passent là-bas, l'une à l'autre pressée.
La jeune m'a giflé, la vieille m'a fessé.

Je vous jure pourtant que je les aimais bien;
Mais constamment, j'avais le besoin bénin
D'exiger trop d'amour: ses larmes et son sein.

Je vous jure, monsieur, qu'elles m'ont bien aimé.
Ça n'est certes pas leur faute à toutes les deux
Si sans cesse je voulais être plus heureux.

C'est ma mère, monsieur, avec ma fiancée.

Pour moi, elles ne sont qu'un même être et leurs charmes
Sont égaux ayant fait verser les mêmes larmes:
Ma mère a pleuré sur moi, qui sanglotais

Pour l'autre, refusant d'être à moi tout à fait;
Je ne sais pas lequel de nous trois fut blessé . . .
C'est ma mère, monsieur, avec ma fiancée.

THE MADMAN SPEAKS

There goes my mother, Sir, with my fiancée.
There they go, arm in arm.
The young woman slapped me; the old woman spanked me.

I swear to you I loved them both;
But I always had the benign need to ask for
Too much love: her tears, and her breast.

I swear to you they loved me well.
Surely it's not their fault
That I always wanted more.

Yes, Sir, that's my mother with my fiancée.

For me they are one and the same person, their charms
Are equal, having made me shed the same tears.
My mother wept over me, while I was sobbing

Over the other one, refusing to be altogether mine;
I don't know which of the three of us was most hurt . . .
There goes my mother, Sir, with my fiancée.

UN SEUL ÊTRE

I

A fait fondre la neige pure,
A fait naître des fleurs dans l'herbe
Et le soleil est délivré.

Ô! fille des saisons variées,
Tes pieds m'attachent à la terre
Et je l'aime toute l'année.

Notre amour rit de ce printemps
Comme de toute ta beauté,
Comme de toute ta bonté.

II

Flûte et violon,
Le rythme d'une chanson claire
Enlève nos deux coeurs pareils
Et les mouettes de la mer.

Oublie nos gestes séparés,
Le rire des sons s'éparpille,
Notre rêve est réalisé.

Nous posséderons l'lhorizon,
La bonne terre qui nous porte
Et l'espace frais et profond,
Flûte et violon.

A SINGLE BEING

I

Has made the pure snow melt,
Caused flowers to be born among the grasses
And released the sun.

Oh! daughter of varied seasons,
Your feet attach me to the earth
And I love it all year long.

Our love laughs with this springtime
As it does for all your beauty,
For all your goodness.

II

Flute and violin,
The rhythm of a clear song
Raises our two like hearts
And the seagulls from the sea.

Forget our separate gestures,
The laughter of sounds scatters,
Our dream is realized.

We shall possess the horizon,
The good earth that carries us,
And the fresh deep space,
Flute and violin.

III

Que te dire encore, amie?
Le matin, dans le jardin,
Le rossignol avale la fraîcheur.
Le jour s'installe en nous
Et nous va jusqu'au coeur.

Le jour s'installe en nous.
Et tout le matin, cherchant le soleil,
L'oiseau s'engourdit sur les branches fines.
Et fuyant le travail, nous allons au soleil,
Avec des yeux contents et des membres légers.

Tu connais le retour, amie,
C'est entre nous que l'oiseau chante,
Le ciel s'orne de son vol,
Le ciel devenu sombre
Et la verdure sombre.

IV

La mer tout entière rayonne,
La mer tout entière abandonne
La terre et son obscur fardeau.

Rêve d'un monde disparu
Dont tu conserves la vertu
Ou rêve plutôt

Que tu m'as gardé sur les flots
Que la lumière . . . Et sous le soleil
Le vent qui s'en va de la terre immense.

III

What more can I tell you, my love?
In the morning, in the garden,
The skylark swallows the freshness.
Day occupies us
Touches our hearts.

Day pervades us
And all morning, looking for the sun,
The bird becomes quiet on delicate branches.
Fleeing work, we go towards the sunlight
Eyes content and light of limb.

You know the return, my love,
The bird sings with us,
The sky is adorned with its flight,
The sky having darkened
All the green darkened.

IV

The whole sea shines
The whole sea abandons
The earth and its obscure burden.

Dream of a world disappeared
Whose virtue you conserve
Or the dream

That you kept me on these waves
That the light . . . And under the sun,
The wind leaves the immense land.

POUR VIVRE ICI

Ton rire est comme un tourbillon de feuilles mortes
Froissant l'air chaud, l'enveloppant, quand vient la pluie.
Amer, tu annules toute tragédie,
Et ton souci d'être un homme, ton rire l'emporte.

Je voudrais t'enfermer avec ta vieille peine
Abandonnée, qui te tient si bien quitte,
Entre les murs nombreux, entre les ciels nombreux
De ma tristesse et de notre raison.

Là, tu retrouverais tant d'autres hommes,
Tant d'autres vies et tant d'espoirs
Que tu serais forcé de voir
Et de te souvenir que tu a su mentir . . .

Ton rire est comme un tourbillon de feuilles mortes.

* * * *

Le vent passe en les branches mortes
Comme ma pensée en les livres,
Et je suis là, sans voix, sans rien,
Et ma chambre s'emplit de ma fenêtre ouverte.

En promenades, en repos, en regards
Pour de l'ombre ou de la lumière
Ma vie s'en va, avec celle des autres.

Le soir vient, sans voix, sans rien.
Je reste là, me cherchant un désir, un plaisir;
Et, vain, je n'ai qu'à m'étonner d'avoir eu à subir
Ma douleur, comme un peu de soleil dans l'eau froide.

TO LIVE HERE[1]

Your laughter is like a whirlwind of autumn leaves
Chafing against the warm air, enveloping it, when rain comes.
Bitter, you annul every tragedy,
Your laughter gets the better of your concern to become a man.

I should like to shut you in with your old suffering
Cast off, which let you off so easy,
Between the many walls, the many skies
Of my sorrow and our reason.

There you would find again so many others
So many other lives and hopes
You would be forced to see
To remember that you knew how to lie . . .

Your laughter is like a whirlwind of autumn leaves.

*   *   *   *

The wind passes through dead branches
Like my thoughts in books,
There I am, voiceless, empty handed,
And my room is filled by my open window.

Strolling, taking it easy, looking around
For shadow or light,
My life goes along with the lives of others.

Evening comes, voiceless, nothing there.
I stay, looking for some desire, some pleasure;
In vain, I can only be astonished at having felt
My pain like a little sunlight in the cold water.

---

[1] These two poems were probably written near the time of Eluard's marriage to Gala on February 21, 1917 while on three-day leave from duty at the front lines. The second poem may refer to his hospitalization for severe bronchitis in March and May of that year.

André Lhote. Reclining figure and dog. Ink drawing for
Les Animaux et leurs hommes, 1920. Coll. Musée Saint Denis.

II

1920 - 1938

ENTRE LES DEUX GUERRES
BETWEEN THE TWO WARS

PRÉFACE

Qu'une force honnête nous revienne.

Quelques poètes, quelques constructeurs qui vécurent jeunes nous l'avaient déjà enseigné.

Connaissons ce dont nous sommes capables.

La beauté ou la laideur ne nous paraissent pas nécessaires. Nous nous sommes toujours autrement souciés de la puissance ou de la grace, de la douceur ou de la brutalité, de la simplicité ou du nombre.

La vanité qui pousse l'homme à déclarer ceci beau ou laid, et à prendre parti, est à la base de l'erreur raffinée de plusieurs époques littéraires, de leur exaltation sentimentale et du désordre qui en résulta.

Essayons, c'est difficile, de rester absolument purs. Nous nous apercevrons alors de tout ce qui nous lie.

Et le langage déplaisant qui suffit aux bavards, langage aussi mort que les couronnes à nos fronts semblables, réduisons-le, transformons-le en un langage charmant, véritable, de commun échange entre nous.

Pour moi, rien ne me semble meilleur signe de cette volonté que ce poème écrit depuis que je songe à cette page d'ouverture:

PREFACE

May an honest strength return to us.

A few poets, builders, ever youthful, had already shown us the way.

Let's be aware of what we are capable of doing.

Beauty or ugliness do not seem necessary to us. Rather, we have always been otherwise concerned with power or grace, gentleness or brutality, with simplicity or multiplicity.

Vanity, which leads one to declare something beautiful or ugly, and to take sides, is responsible for the refined error of several literary ages, for their sentimental exaltation and the disorder which ensued.

Let us try to remain absolutely pure, however difficult that may be. Then we shall become aware of all which brings us together.

As for the displeasing language which satisfies gossips, that language as dead as the crowns on our like brows; let's reduce and transform it into a truthful language of charm, of common exchange among us.

For my part, nothing seems to be a better sign of this intention than the poem written as I have been imagining this opening page:

SALON

Amour des fantaisies permises
Du soleil,
Des citrons,
Du mimosa léger.
Clarté des moyens employés:
Vitre claire,
Patience
Et vase à transpercer.

Du soleil, des citrons, du mimosa léger
Au fort de la fragilité
Du verre qui contient
Cet or en boules,
Cet or qui roule.

ANIMAL RIT

Le monde rit,
Le monde est heureux, content et joyeux.
La bouche s'ouvre, ouvre ses ailes et retombe.
Les bouches jeunes retombent,
Les bouches vieilles retombent.

Un animal rit aussi,
Étendant la joie de ses contorsions.
Dans tous les endroits de la terre
Le poil remue, la laine danse
Et les oiseaux perdent leurs plumes.

Un animal rit aussi
Et saute loin de lui-même.
Le monde rit,
Un animal rit aussi,
Un animal s'enfuit.

SALON

Love of permitted fantasies
Of sunshine,
Of lemons,
Of airy mimosa.
Clarity of the means used:
A clear window pane,
Patience,
And the vessel to be pierced.

Sunshine, lemons, light mimosa
In the stronghold of the fragility
Of glass containing
This gold in balls,
This rolling gold.

AN ANIMAL LAUGHS

The world laughs,
The world is happy, content, joyful.
The mouth opens, opens its wings, falls again.
Young mouths fall again
Old mouths fall again.

An animal laughs too,
Stretching the joy of its contortions
Everywhere in the land
Fur is ruffled, fleece dances
And birds lose their feathers.

An animal laughs too,
Jumps away from himself.
The world is laughing,
An animal is laughing too,
An animal runs away.

Les animaux et leurs hommes, les hommes et leurs animaux [1920]

CHEVAL

Cheval seul, cheval perdu,
Malade de la pluie, vibrant d'insectes,
Cheval seul, vieux cheval.

. . . .

Et, fidèle aux cailloux,
Cheval seul attend la nuit
Pour n'être pas obligé
De voir clair et de se sauver.

POULE

Hélas! ma soeur, bête bête,
Ce n'est pas à cause de ton chant
De ton chant pour l'oeuf
Que l'homme te croit bonne.

POISSON

Les poissons, les nageurs, les bateaux
Transforment l'eau.
L'eau est douce et ne bouge
Que pour ce qui la touche.

Le poisson avance
Comme un doigt dans un gant,
Le nageur danse lentement
Et la voile respire.

Mais l'eau douce bouge
Pour ce qui la touche,
Pour le poisson, pour le nageur, pour le bateau
Qu'elle porte
Et qu'elle emporte.

HORSE

Horse alone, lost,
Sick from the rain, vibrating with insects,
Lonely old horse.
. . . .
Faithful to the pebbles
Lonely horse awaits the night
To avoid having to see danger
And run away.

HEN

Alas! my sister, silly beast,
It's not for your clucking song
Over the egg
That men hold you in esteem.

FISH

Fish, swimmers and boats
Transform the water.
Water is soft, yielding
Only to what touches it.

The fish advances
Like a finger in a glove,
The swimmer slowly dances,
The sail breathes.

Yet gentle water yields
To whatever touches it,
For the fish, the swimmer, the boat
That it bears
And carries away.

OISEAU

Charmée . . . Oh! pauvre fille!
Les oiseaux mettent en désordre
Le soleil aveuglant du toit,
Les oiseaux jouent à remplacer
Le soleil plus léger que l'huile
Qui coule entre nous.

CHIEN

Chien chaud,
Tout entier dans la voix, dans les gestes
De ton maître,
Prends la vie comme le vent,
Avec ton nez.
Reste tranquille.

CHAT

Pour ne poser qu'un doigt dessus
Le chat est bien trop grosse bête.
Sa queue rejoint sa tête,
Il tourne dans ce cercle
Et se répond à la caresse.

Mais, la nuit, l'homme voit ses yeux
Dont la pâleur est le seul don.
Ils sont trop gros pour qu'il les cache
Et trop lourds pour le vent perdu du rêve.

Quand le chat danse
C'est pour isoler sa prison
Et quand il pense
C'est jusqu'aux murs de ses yeux.

BIRD

Charmed . . . Oh! poor girl!
The birds disturb
The blinding sunshine on the roof,
Birds play at replacing
The sunshine lighter than the oil
That flows between us.

DOG

Warm pup,
Living by the voice and gestures
Of your master,
Take life like the wind,
With your nose.
And be still.

CAT

Putting only a finger on it we know
The cat is much too big.
Its tail joins its head,
It turns in a circle
And responds to a caress.

But at night we see its eyes
A pale glow their only attribute.
They are too big to be concealed
Too heavy for the lost wind of a dream.

The cat dances
To isolate its prison
It thinks as far
As the limits of its eyes.

MODÈLE

Les filets des arbres ont pris beaucoup d'oiseaux
Natures
Les pattes des oiseaux ont pris les branches sûres
A leurs os.

HOMME UTILE

Tu ne peux plus travailler. Rêve,
Les yeux ouverts, les mains ouvertes
Dans le désert,
Dans le désert qui joue
Avec les animaux — les inutiles.

Après l'ordre, après le désordre,
Dans les champs plats, les forets creuses,
Dans la mer lourde et claire,
Un animal passe — et ton rêve
Est bien le rêve du repos.

PLUMES

L'homme voudrait être sorti
D'un fouillis d'ailes.
Très haut, le vent coule en criant
Le long d'une aile.

Mais la mère n'était pas là
Quand le nid s'envola
Mais le ciel battait de l'aile
Quand le nid s'envola.

MODEL

The trees' netting took in many birds
Naturally
The birds' feet connected the certain branches
To their bones.

UTILITARIAN MAN

You can't work any more. Dream,
Open-eyed, openhanded
In the wilderness
In the wilderness that plays
With the animals — the useless ones.

Following order and disorder,
On the level plains, in deep forests,
In the weighty, clear ocean,
An animal passes by — and your dream
Is surely one of repose.

FEATHERS

Man would like to have emerged
From a mess of wings.
Way up there, the wind flows howling
Along the length of a wing.

But the mother wasn't there
When the nest flew away,
And the sky was beating its wings
When the nest blew away.

Les animaux et leurs hommes, les hommes et leurs animaux [1920]

Et, désespoir du sol,
L'homme est couché dans ses paroles,
Au long des branches mortes,
Dans des coquilles d'oeufs.

MOUILLÉ

La pierre rebondit sur l'eau
La fumée n'y pénètre pas.
L'eau, telle une peau
Que nul ne peut blesser
Est caressée
Par l'homme et par le poisson.

Claquant comme corde d'arc,
Le poisson, quand l'homme l'attrape,
Meurt, ne pouvant avaler
Cette planète d'air et de lumière.

Et l'homme sombre au fond des eaux
Pour le poisson
Ou pour la solitude amère
De l'eau souple et toujours close.

PATTE

Le chat s'établit dans la nuit pour crier,
Dans l'air libre, dans la nuit, le chat crie.
Et, triste, à hauteur d'homme,
l'homme entend son cri.

And to the earth's dismay,
Man lies among his words,
Along dead branches,
In empty shells.

DAMPENED

The stone rebounds on the water
Smoke does not penetrate there.
Water, like a skin
None can wound,
Is caressed
By man and by fish.

Snapping like a bowstring,
The fish, when caught by the man,
Expires, unable to swallow
This planet of air and light.

But man sinks to the waters' depths
For the fish,
Or for the bitter solitude
Of the supple, unyielding waters.

PAW

The cat settles down in the night to yowl,
In the free air of night, the cat meows.
And sorrowful, standing at a man's height,
Man hears its cry.

POULE [2]

Il faut que la poule ponde:
Poule avec ses fruits mûrs,
Poule avec notre gain.

FUIR

L'araignée rapide,
Pieds et mains de la peur,
Est arrivée.

L'araignée,
Heureuse de son poids,
Reste immobile
Comme le plomb du fil à plomb.

Et quand elle repart,
Brisant tous les fils,
C'est la poursuite dans le vide
Qu'il faut imaginer,

Toute chose détruite.

HEN [2]

The hen must lay:
The hen with its ripe fruits
Hen for our profit

TO FLEE

The speedy spider,
With feet and hands of fear,
Has arrived.

The spider,
Happy with her weight,
Is motionless
Like the sinker at the end of the line.

And when she takes off again,
Breaking all the threads,
It's a chase in space
We must imagine,

Everything destroyed.

Les nécessités de la vie et les conséquences des rêves [1921]

précédé

d'Exemples

L'erreur singulière de Victor Hugo, de Stéphane Mallarmé et de Mme Mathieu de Noailles nous peut donner à penser, plus loin, que les mots, loin qu'ils portent goût, odeur ou musique, le sens même ne leur est pas une propriété tellement assurée qu'ils ne la laissent aller aussitôt que l'écrivain les néglige, ou les accueille sans brutalité d'esprit, ou bien encore ne tient pas compte de leurs veines, fil et sorte particulière de résistance.

Pour les proverbes, exemples et autres mots à jamais marqués d'une première trouvaille, combien ce vide autour d'eux les fait plus absurdes et purs, pareillement difficiles à inventer, à maintenir. J'aime que Paul Eluard les reçoive tels, ou les recherche. Ensuite commencent ses poèmes.

— Jean Paulhan

The necessities of life and the consequences of dreams [1921]

preceeded by

Examples

*The singular error of Victor Hugo, Stephane Mallarmé and
Mme Mathieu de Noailles may lead us to think, at this distance, that
for words, far from having taste, aroma or music, meaning itself is not
an assured property . . . when the writer neglects them, or welcomes
them without discrimination, or is unaware of their veins, thread and
particular resistance.*

*As for proverbs, exemplary tales and other words forever
marked by their first discovery, how this empty space around them
renders them more absurd and untouched, equally difficult to invent,
to maintain. I am pleased that Paul Eluard receives them as such, or
searches for them. Here then begin his poems.*

— Jean Paulhan

Exemples

QUATRE GOSSES

Le gourmand dépouillé,
Gonflant ses joues,
Avalant une fleur,
Odorante peau intérieure.

Enfant sage,
Sifflet,
Bouche forcément rose,
Bouche légère sous la tête lourde,
Un à dix, dix à un.

L'orphelin,
Le sein qui le nourrit enveloppé de noir
Ne le lavera pas.
Sale
Comme une forêt de nuit d'hiver.

Mort,
Les belles dents, mais les beaux yeux immobiles,
Fixes!
Quelle mouche de sa vie
Est la mère des mouches de sa mort?

Examples

FOUR CHILDREN

The gourmand down to the bone,
Blowing up his cheeks,
Swallowing a flower,
Sweet smelling inner skin.

Nice child,
A whistle,
A rosy mouth, of course,
Light mouth under the heavy brow.
One to ten, ten to one.

The orphan, the breast that nurses him wrapped in black
Will not wash him,
Dirty
As a forest on a winter's night.

A dead one,
White teeth, but his beautiful eyes still,
fixed!
What fly in his life
Is the mother of the flies of his death?

AUTRES GOSSES

Confidence:
"Petit enfant de mes cinq sens
Et de ma douceur."
Berçons les amours,
Nous aurons des enfants sages.
Bien accompagnés,
Nous ne craindrons plus rien sur terre,
Bonheur, félicité, prudence,
Les amours

Et ce bond d'âge en âge,
Du rang d'enfant à celui de vieillard,
Ne nous réduira pas
(Confidence).

OTHER CHILDREN

Confidence:
"Little child of my five senses
and of my tenderness."
Let us cradle our loves,
We will have good children.
Well cared for,
We will fear nothing on earth,
Happiness, good fortune, prudence,
Our loves

And this leap from age to age,
From the order of a child to that of an old man,
Will not diminish us.
(Confidence).

Conséquences des Rêves

Le château faisait le tour de la ville. Au fond, les habitants s'aimaient bien. En haine nécessaire et périodique, ils ne se passaient l'épée qu'autour du corps.

LA VIE, grand-père, père et fils, trois hommes, d'évidence en évidence en évidence.

Ombres sans ombres. Le soleil commença sa promenade dans la place. Des plantes et des fidèles accompagnaient son chant. Des nuages sur la tête et les pieds dans la poussière, grandirait-il?

Nous, nous étions à l'ombre des anges, l'amour ancien.

Consequences of Dreams

The castle circled the city. In their hearts, the inhabitants liked each other well enough. With necessary, recurring hatred, they swung their swords only around their own bodies.

LIFE, grandfather, father and son, three men, from evidence to evidence to evidence.

Shadows without shadows. The sun began its promenade in the city square. Some plants and a few of the faithful accompanied its song. With clouds on its head and its feet in the dust, would it grow then?

As for the rest of us, we were in the shadow of the angels, ancient love.

René Magritte. The poet and his shadow. Portrait of Eluard.
Ink drawing *Les nécessités de la vie et les conséquences des rêves.*
1946 edition. Coll. Musée Saint Denis.

René Magritte. Ink drawing for *Les nécessités de la vie et les conséquences des rêves*, 1946 edition. Coll. Musée Saint Denis.

Mourir de ne pas mourir   [1924]

Je meurs...

L'AMOUREUSE

Elle est debout sur mes paupières
Et ses cheveux sont dans les miens,
Elle a la forme de mes mains,
Elle a la couleur de mes yeux,
Elle s'engloutit dans mon ombre

Comme une pierre sur le ciel.
Elle a toujours les yeux ouverts
Et ne me laisse pas dormir.
Ses rêves en pleine lumière
Font s'évaporer les soleils,
Me font rire, pleurer et rire,
Parler sans avoir rien à dire.

LE SOURD ET L'AVEUGLE

Gagnerons-nous la mer avec des cloches
Dans nos poches, avec le bruit de la mer
Dans la mer, ou bien serons-nous les porteurs
D'une eau plus pure et silencieuse?

L'eau se frottant les mains aiguise des couteaux
Les guerriers ont trouvé leurs armes dans les flots
Et le bruit de leurs coups est semblable à celui
Des rochers défonçant dans la nuit les bateaux.

C'est la tempête et le tonnerre. Pourquoi pas le silence
Du déluge, car nous avons en nous tout l'espace rêvé
Pour le plus grand silence et nous respirerons
Comme le vent des mers terribles, comme le vent

Qui rampe lentement sur tous les horizons.

Dying from not dying [1924]

                                          I am dying....[1]
THE LOVER

She is standing on my eyelids,
Her hair mingles with mine,
She takes on the shape of my hands,
She is the color of my eyes,
She is absorbed by my shadow
Like a stone against the sky.

Her eyes are forever open
She doesn't let me sleep.
Her dreams in the light of day
Make the suns evaporate,
Make me laugh, cry, and laugh again,
And babble on with nothing to say.

THE DEAF AND THE BLIND

Will we get down to the sea with bells
In our pockets, with the sound of the sea
In the sea, or will we be the carriers
Of purer, silent waters?

Water rubbing its hands sharpens knives
Warriers have found weapons in the waves
And the sound of their blows is like
Rocks shattering boats in the night.

That's the storm and thunder. Why not the silence
Of the flood, for in us we have all the space we dreamed of
For the most complete silence and we shall breathe
Like the wind of the terrible seas, the wind

That slowly crawls up all the horizons.

---

[1] This book appeared the day following Eluard's unannounced departure
from Marseilles for the Far East, where Gala and Max Ernst joined him
later; he dedicated this "last book" to Breton "to simplify everything."

Mourir de ne pas mourir [1924]

LE JEU DE CONSTRUCTION

L'homme s'enfuit, le cheval tombe,
La porte ne peut pas s'ouvrir,
L'oiseau se taît, creusez sa tombe,
Le silence le fait mourir.

Un papillon sur une branche
Attend patiemment l'hiver,
Son coeur est lourd, la branche penche,
La branche se plie comme un ver.

Pourquoi pleurer la fleur séchée
Et pourquoi pleurer les lilas?
Pourquoi pleurer la rose d'ambre?
Pourquoi pleurer la pensée tendre?
Pourquoi chercher la fleur cachée
    Si l'on n'a pas de récompense?

       — Mais pour ça, ça et ça.

GIORGIO DE CHIRICO

Un mur dénonce un autre mur
Et l'ombre me défend de mon ombre peureuse.
O tour de mon amour autour de mon amour,
Tous les murs filaient blanc autour de mon silence.

Toi, que défendais-tu? Ciel insensible et pur
Tremblant tu m'abritais. La lumière en relief
Sur le ciel qui n'est plus le miroir du soleil,
Les étoiles de jour parmi les feuilles vertes,

Le souvenir de ceux qui parlaient sans savoir,
Maîtres de ma faiblesse et je suis à leur place
Avec des yeux d'amour et des mains trop fidèles
Pour dépeupler un monde dont je suis absent.

Dying from not dying [1924]

THE GAME OF BUILDING

The man flees, the horse falls,
The door can't be opened,
The bird grows silent, dig his grave,
The silence is killing him.

A butterfly on a branch
Patiently awaits winter,
Heavy-hearted; the branch leans down,
The branch bends like a worm.

Why do we weep for the dried flower
Why do we weep for the lilacs?
Why do we mourn the amber rose?
Why cry over thoughts so tender?
Why do we seek the hidden flower —
    If there is no recompense?

        — Well, for one reason or another.

GIORGIO DE CHIRICO[1]

One wall denies another
And the shadow protects me from my fearful shadow.
Oh tower of my love circling my love,
All the walls were moving white around my silence.

And what were you protecting? Pure, unfeeling sky,
Trembling, you sheltered me. Light in relief
Against the sky — no longer the sun's mirror —
Stars of day among the green leaves,

Memory of those who spoke unknowing,
Masters of my inclination I am with them
With loving eyes and hands too faithful
To remove them from a world I left behind.

---

[1] Italian futurist of surreal tendencies, who painted lonely cityscapes.

51

Mourir de ne pas mourir [1924]

NUDITÉ DE LA VÉRITÉ

Je le sais bien.

Le désespoir n'a pas d'ailes,
L'amour non plus,
Pas de visage,
Ne parlent pas,
Je ne bouge bas,
Je ne les regarde pas,
Je ne leur parle pas
Mais je suis bien aussi vivant que mon amour
            et que mon désespoir.

TA FOI

Suis-je autre chose que ta force?
Ta force dans tes bras,
Ta tête dans tes bras,
Ta force dans le ciel décomposé,
Ta tête lamentable,
Ta tête que je porte.
Tu ne joueras plus avec moi,
Héroïne perdue,
Ma force bouge dans tes bras.

Dying from not dying [1924]

THE NAKED TRUTH

I know it well.

Despair has no wings,
Nor has love,
They have no face,
They do not speak,
I don't move,
I don't look at them,
I won't speak to them
Yet surely I am as alive as my love
    — and my despair.

YOUR FAITH

Am I anything else but your strength?
Your strength in your arms,
Your head in your arms,
Your strength in the sky decomposed,
Your lamentable head,
Your head which I bear.
You won't play with me any more,
Lost heroine,
My strength moves in your arms.

L'amour la poésie [1929]

PREMIÈREMENT

À Gala ce livre sans fin

I

À haute voix
L'amour agile se leva
Avec de si brillants éclats
Que dans son grenier le cerveau
Eut peur de tout avouer.

À haute voix
Tous les corbeaux du sang couvrirent
La mémoire d'autres naissances
Puis renversés dans la lumière
L'avenir roué de baisers.

Injustice impossible un seul être est au monde
L'amour choisit l'amour sans changer de visage.

II

Ses yeux sont des tours de lumière
Sous le front de sa nudité.

À fleur de transparence
Les retours de pensées
Annulent les mots qui sont sourds.

Elle efface toutes les images
Elle éblouit l'amour et ses ombres rétives
Elle aime — elle aime à s'oublier.

Love ~ Poetry [1929]

FIRST OF ALL

To Gala this book without end

I

Outloud
Agile love got up
With such sparkling brilliance
That the brain in its attic
Was afraid to confess it all.

Outloud
All the crows of the blood covered up
The memory of other births,
Then upset in the light
The future worn down by kisses.

Impossible injustice a single being is in the world
Love chooses love without changing its countenance.

II

Her eyes are towers of light
Under the brow of her nudity.

Surfacing transparent
Returning thoughts
Cancel the muffled words.

She blots out all the images
She dazzles love and its untamed shadows
She's in love — she loves to forget herself.

III

Les représentants tout-puissants du désir
Des yeux graves nouveau-nés
Pour supprimer la lumière
L'arc de tes seins tendu par un aveugle
Qui se souvient de tes mains
Ta faible chevelure
Est dans le fleuve ignorant de ta tête
Caresses au fil de la peau
Et ta bouche qui se taît
Peut prouver l'impossible.

IV

Je te l'ai dit pour les nuages
Je te l'ai dit pour l'arbre de la mer
Pour chaque vague pour les oiseaux dans les feuilles
Pour les cailloux du bruit
Pour les mains familières
Pour l'oeil qui devient visage ou paysage
Et le sommeil lui rend le ciel de sa couleur
Pour toute la nuit bue
Pour la grille des routes
Pour la fenêtre ouverte pour un front découvert
Je te l'ai dit pour tes pensées pour tes paroles
Toute caresse toute confiance se survivent.

V

Plus c'était un baiser
Moins les mains sur les yeux
Les halos de la lumière
Aux lèvres de l'horizon
Et des tourbillons de sang
Qui se livraient au silence.

III

The all-powerful representatives of desire
Serious eyes newly born
To put out the light
The curve of your breasts held up by a blind man
Who remembers your hands
Your light flowing hair
Is in the unconscious river of your head
Caresses over your skin
Your mouth now silent
Can prove the impossible.

IV

I told you this for the clouds
I told you this for the tree of the sea
For every wave for the birds in the leaves
For the pebbles of sound
For familiar hands
For the eye that becomes a face or a landscape
And sleep which gives the sky its color
For the whole night imbibed
For the network of roads
For the window opened for a brow revealed
I told you this for your thoughts and your words
Every caress every confidence outlast themselves

V

The more profound the kiss
The less we covered our eyes
Halos of light
At the lips of the horizon
Whirlpools of blood
Surrendered to silence.

VI

Toi la seule et j'entends les herbes de ton rire
Toi c'est ta tête qui t'enlève
Et du haut des dangers de mort
Sous les globes brouillés de la pluie des vallées
Sous la lumière lourde sous le ciel de terre
Tu enfantes la chute.

Les oiseaux ne sont plus un abri suffisant
Ni la paresse ni la fatigue
Le souvenir des bois et des ruisseaux fragiles
Au matin des caprices
Au matin des caresses visibles
Au grand matin de l'absence la chute.
Les barques de tes yeux s'égarent
Dans la dentelle des disparitions
Le gouffre est dévoilée aux autres de l'éteindre
Les ombres que tu crées n'ont pas droit à la nuit.

VII

La terre est bleue comme une orange
Jamais une erreur les mots ne mentent pas
Ils ne vous donnent plus à chanter
Au tour des baisers de s'entendre
Les fous et les amours
Elle sa bouche d'alliance
Tous les secrets tous les sourires
Et quels vêtements d'indulgence
À la croire toute nue.

Les guêpes fleurissent vert
L'aube se passe autour du cou
Un collier de fenêtres
Des ailes couvrent les feuilles
Tu as toutes les joies solaires
Tout le soleil sur la terre
Sur les chemins de ta beauté.

VI

You the one and only I hear your laughter like blades of grass
You it's your head that carries you off
And from the heights of the dangers of death
Under foggy globes of valley rain
Under the heavy illumination under an earthen sky
You engender the fall.

The birds are no longer adequate shelter
Nor is lethargy nor fatigue
The memory of woods and fragile streams
In the morning of whims
In the morning of visible caresses
At the high noon of absence the downfall.
The vessels of your eyes
In the intricacies of disappearances
The abyss is unveiled others may put it out
The shadows you created have no right to the night.

VII

The earth is blue like an orange
There's no mistake words don't lie
They don't give you anything to sing about
When it's time to hear kisses
The madmen and our loves
She with her mouth of alliance
All the secrets all the smiles
And such indulgent clothing
Making one think she is naked.

The wasps blossom green
Dawn wraps a necklace
Of windows round its neck
Wings cover leaves
You have all the solar joys
All the sunshine on earth
On the paths of your beauty.

L'amour la poésie *[1929]*

VIII

Mon amour pour avoir figuré mes désirs
Mis tes lèvres au ciel de tes mots comme un astre
Tes baisers dans la nuit vivante
Et le sillage de tes bras autour de moi
Comme une flamme en signe de conquête
Mes rêves sont au monde
Clairs et perpétuels.

Et quand tu n'es pas là
Je rêve que je dors je rêve que je rêve.

IX

Où la vie se contemple tout est submergé
Monté les couronnes d'oubli
Les vertiges au coeur des métamorphoses
D'une écriture d'algues solaires
L'amour et l'amour.

Tes mains font le jour dans l'herbe
Tes yeux font l'amour en plein jour
Les sourires par la taille
Et tes lèvres par les ailes
Tu prends la place des caresses
Tu prends la place des réveils.
. . . .

Love ~ Poetry   [1929]

VIII

My love for having taken the form of my desires
For having put your lips into the sky of your words like a star
Your kisses in the living night
And the furrowing of your arms around me
Like a flame a sign of conquest
My dreams are of this world
Clear and enduring.

And when you are away
I dream that I sleep I dream that I dream

IX

When life looks within all is submerged
Raised are the crowns of oblivion
Vertigo at the heart of metamorphoses
In the handwriting of solar algae
Love and love.

Your hands make day in the grass
Your eyes make love in broad daylight
Smiles by your waist
And your lips by the wings
You take the place of caresses
You take the place of awakenings.

. . . .

XI

Elle ne sait pas tendre des pièges
Elle a les yeux sur sa beauté
Si simple si simple séduire
Et ce sont ses yeux qui l'enchaînent
Et c'est sur moi qu'elle s'appuie
Et c'est sur elle qu'elle jette
Le filet volant des caresses.

XII

Le mensonge menaçant les ruses dures et glissantes
Des bouches au fond des puits des yeux au fond des nuits
Et des vertus subites des filets à jeter au hasard
Les envies d'inventer d'admirables béquilles
Des faux des pièges entre les corps entre les lèvres
Des patiences massives des impatiences calculées
Tout ce qui s'impose et qui règne
Entre la liberté d'aimer
Et celle de ne pas aimer
Tout ce que tu ne connais pas.

XIII

Amoureuse au secret derrière ton sourire
Toute nue les mots d'amour
Découvrent tes seins et ton cou
Et tes hanches et tes paupières
Découvrant toutes les caresses
Pour que les baisers dans tes yeux
Ne montrent que toi tout entière.

. . . .

XI

She doesn't know how to set traps
She sees her beauty
So easy so easy to seduce
And her own eyes ensnare her
And it's on me that she leans
And over herself that she casts
The flying net of caresses.

XII

The menacing lie the hard and slippery ploys
Of mouths at the bottom of the wells of eyes
        in the depths of the night
And sudden virtues of nets cast out by chance
Wanting to invent admirable crutches
Fakes traps between bodies between lips
Massive patience calculated impatience
All that imposes and reigns
Between the freedom of loving
And that of not loving
Everything you do not know.

XIII

In love in the secret behind your smile
Naked words of love
Uncover your breasts your neck
Your hips and your eyelids
Discovering all the caresses
So that the kisses in your eyes
Disclose only you all together.

XIV

Le sommeil a pris ton empreinte
Et la colore de tes yeux

XV

Elle se penche sur moi
Le coeur ignorant
Pour voir si je l'aime
Elle a confiance elle oublie
Sous les nuages de ses paupières
Sa tête s'endort dans mes mains
Où sommes-nous
Ensemble inséparables
Vivants vivants
Vivant vivante
Et ma tête roule en ses rêves.

XVI

Bouches gourmandes des couleurs
Et les baisers qui les dessinent
Flamme feuille l'eau langoureuse
Une aile les tient dans sa paume
Un rire les renverse.

XVII

D'une seule caresse
Je te fais briller de tout ton éclat.

. . . .

XIV

Sleep has taken your imprint
And gives it the color of your eyes.

XV

She leans over me
Unknowing heart
To see if I love her
She is confident she forgets
Under the clouds of her eyes
Her head falls asleep in my hands
Where are we
Together inseparable
Alive both of us
Each of us alive
And my head rolls in her dreams.

XVI

Greedy mouths of colors
And kisses that delineate them
Flame leaf languid water
A wing holds them in its plan
A chuckle topples them over.

XVII

With a single caresse
I make you shine in all your splendor.

. . . .

COMME UNE IMAGE

I

Je cache les sombres trésors
Des retraites inconnues
Le coeur des forêts le sommeil
D'une fusée ardente
L'horizon nocturne
Qui me couronne
Je vais la tête la première
Saluant d'un secret nouveau
La naissance des images.

. . . .

XIV

À l'assaut des jardins
Les saisons sont partout à la fois
Passion de l'été pour l'hiver
Et la tendresse des deux autres
Les souvenirs comme des plumes
Les arbres ont brisé le ciel
Un beau chêne gâché de brume
La vie des oiseaux ou la vie des plumes
Et tout un panache frivole
Avec de souriantes craintes
Et la solitude bavarde.

LIKE AN IMAGE

I

I hide the dark treasures
Of unknown retreats
The heart of forests the sleep
Of a burning rocket
The nocturnal horizon
That crowns me
I go head first
Greeting with a new secret
The birth of images.

. . . .

XIV

In their assault on the gardens
The seasons are everywhere at once
The passion of summer for winter
And the tenderness of the two others
Memories like feathers
The trees have shattered the sky
A fine oak spoiled with fog
The life of birds or the life of feathers
And a whole frivolous panache
With smiling fears
And gossiping solitude.

Facile *[1935]*

TU TE LÈVES L'EAU SE DÉPLIE

Tu te lèves l'eau se déplie
Tu te couches l'eau s'épanouit

Tu es l'eau détournée de ses abîmes
Tu es la terre qui prend racine
Et sur laquelle tout s'établit

Tu fais des bulles de silence dans le désert des bruits
Tu chantes des hymnes nocturnes sur les cordes de l'arc-en-ciel
Tu es partout tu abolis toutes les routes

Tu sacrifies le temps
À l'éternelle jeunesse de la flamme exacte
Qui voile la nature en la reproduisant

Femme tu mets au monde un corps toujours pareil
Le tien

Tu es la ressemblance.

Easy [1935]

YOU RISE THE WATER UNFOLDS

You rise the water unfolds
You lie down the water expands

You are water diverted from its abysses
You are the earth which takes root
And upon which everything is built

You blow bubbles of silence in the wilderness of noise
You sing nocturnal hymns on the rainbow's strings
You are everywhere you abolish all roads

You sacrifice time
To the eternal youth of the rigorous flame
Which veils nature in reproducing it

Woman you bring into the world a body always the same
Your own

You are resemblance.

La barre d'appui *[1936]*

ET QUEL ÂGE AVEZ-VOUS?

Parlons de la jeunesse
Perdons notre jeunesse
Rions d'elle elle rit
La tête à la renverse
Rire est plus fort que dire

Les formes fines qui nous tentent
Encore
Ces formes hypocrites
Si changeantes si mal fardées
Devant elles
Nos mains de beurre frais
Sont embarrassées
Et nos lèvres de bronze
Immortalisées par le chant
Honteuses
Balbutient des adieux
Incompréhensibles

Une scie qui se brise.

SO HOW OLD ARE YOU?

Let's speak of youth
Let's lose our youth
Let's laugh at it laughing
Head thrown back
Laughing is stronger than speaking

The fine shapes that tempt us
Even now
These hypocritical shapes
So changeable so poorly powdered
Before them
Our hands of fresh butter
Are confused
And our lips of bronze
Immortalized by song
Ashamed
Stammer goodbyes
Incomprehensible

A saw is broken.

Les Yeux Fertiles [1936]

LES YEUX FERTILES

On ne peut me connaître
Mieux que tu me connais

Tes yeux dans lesquels nous dormons
Tous les deux
Ont fait à mes lumières d'homme
Un sort meilleur qu'aux nuits du monde

Tes yeux dans lesquels je voyage
Ont donné aux gestes des routes
Un sens détaché de la terre

Dans tes yeux ceux qui nous révèlent
Notre solitude infinie
Ne sont plus ce qu'ils croyaient être

On ne peut te connaître
Mieux que je te connais.

FERTILE EYES[1]

No one can know me
Better than you

Your eyes where we both
Are sleeping
Have given my man's lights
A destiny better than the world's dark nights

Your eyes where I travel
Have given the roads' gesturing
A sense detached from the earth

In your eyes those who show us
Our infinite solitude
Are no longer what they thought they were

No one can know you
Better than I do.

---

[1] "Fertile eyes" are the eyes of Picasso. Most of these poems were set to music by Francis Poulenc, under the title "Tel jour, telle nuit".

GRAND AIR

La rive des mains tremblantes
Descendait sous la pluie
Un escalier de brumes
Tu sortais toute nue
Faux marbre palpitant
Teint de bon matin
Trésor gardé par des bêtes immenses
Qui gardaient elles du soleil sous leurs ailes
Pour toi
Des bêtes que nous connaissions sans les voir
Par-delà les murs de nos nuits
Par-delà l'horizon de nos baisers
Le rire contagieux des hyènes
Pouvait bien ronger les vieux os
Des êtres qui vivent un par un

Nous jouions au soleil à la pluie à la mer
À n'avoir qu'un regard qu'un ciel et qu'une mer
Les nôtres.

Fertile Eyes [1936]

OPEN AIR

The bank of trembling hands
Was coming down the misty staircase
In the rain
You emerged naked
False marble palpitating
With a fine morning glow
A treasure watched over by huge beasts
That harbored sunshine under their wings
For you
Beasts we recognized yet did not see
Beyond the walls of our nights
Beyond the horizon of our kisses
The contagious laughter of hyenas
Might well gnaw at the old bones
Of solitary beings living one by one

Under the sun in the rain by the sea
We used to play at having one way of seeing
One sky one sea yours and mine.

Les Yeux Fertiles *[1936]*

DURER

Une rafale une seule
D'horizon à horizon
Et ainsi sur toute la terre
Pour balayer la poussière
Les myriades de feuilles mortes
Pour dépouiller tous les arbres
Pour dévaster les cultures
Pour abattre les oiseaux
Pour éparpiller les vagues
Pour détruire les fumées
Pour rompre l'équilibre
Du soleil le plus chaud
Fuyante masse faiblesse
Monde qui ne pèse rien
Monde ancien qui m'ignore
Ombre affolée
Je ne serai plus libre que dans d'autres bras.

TO ENDURE

A squall gusting
From horizon to horizon
Over the whole land
To sweep away the dust
The myriads of dead leaves
To strip the trees
To devastate the crops
To beat down the birds
To scatter the waves
To dissipate the smoke
To break the equilibrium
Of the hottest sun
Fleeing mass frailty
Weightless world
Old world that ignores me
Crazed shadow never will I be free again
Unless in another's arms.

JE CROYAIS LE REPOS POSSIBLE

Une ruine coquille vide
Pleure dans son tablier
Les enfants qui jouent autour d'elle
Font moins de bruit que des mouches

La ruine s'en va à tâtons
Chercher ses vaches dans un pré
J'ai vu le jour je vois cela
Sans en avoir honte

Il est minuit comme une flèche
Dans un coeur à la portée
Des folâtres lueurs nocturnes
Qui contredisent le sommeil.

ONDÉE

Belle sans la terre ferme
Sans parquet sans souliers sans draps
Je te néante.

I THOUGHT REST POSSIBLE

A ruin of an empty shell
Weeps in her apron
The children playing round her
Make less noise than flies

The old ruin goes off feeling her way
To look for her cows in a field
I have seen the light I see all that
Without shame

Midnight strikes like an arrow
In a heart within reach of
Giddy nocturnal lights
That contradict sleep.

DELUGE

Beauty without firm ground
Without wood floors or shoes or sheets
I annihilate you.

HORS DE LA MASSE

Une fenêtre en face
Est un trou noir
Un linge blanc s'en échappe
De perfection en perfection
De ciel en ciel
L'or têtu jette sa semence
Au son crevé des midis creux
Sur la fourchette des putains
Un bec de viande gonfle un air
D'usure et de cendres froides
La solitude des putains

Elles se cassent les vertèbres
A dormir debout et sans rêves
Devant des fênetres ouvertes
Sur l'ombre coriace d'un linge.

BEYOND THE CROWD

The window opposite
Is a black hole
A white curtain flutters there
From perfection to perfection
From sky to sky
Stubborn gold casts its seed
In the dead sound of hollow noons
On the prostitutes' forks
A glob of meat blows up a tune
Of used women and cold ashes
The solitude of whores

They are breaking their vertibrae
Sleeping dreamless on their feet
In front of windows opening onto
The rough shadow of a cloth.

Cours Naturel [1938]

SANS ÂGE

Nous approchons
Dans les forêts
Prenez la rue du matin
Montez les marches de la brume

Nous approchons
La terre en a le coeur crispé

Encore un jour à mettre au monde.

*

Le ciel s'élargira
Nous en avions assez
D'habiter dans les ruines du sommeil
Dans l'ombre basse du repos
De la fatigue de l'abandon

La terre reprendra la forme de nos corps vivants
Le vent nous subira
Le soleil et la nuit passeront dans nos yeux
Sans jamais les changer

Notre espace certain notre air pur est de taille
À combler le retard creusé par l'habitude
Nous aborderons tous une mémoire nouvelle

*

Ô mes frères contraires gardant dans vos prunelles
La nuit infuse et son horreur
Où vous ai-je laissés
Avec vos lourdes mains dans l'huile paresseuse
De vos actes anciens
Avec si peu d'espoir que la mort a raison
Ô mes frères perdus

82

TIMELESS

We are approaching
Through the woods
Take the path of morning
Climb the steps of fog

We are coming closer
The earth holds its breath

Still another day to be born

*

Horizons will widen
We had enough of
Living in the ruins of sleep
In the low shadow of rest
Of fatigue and abandon

The land will once again take on the form
Of our living bodies the wind will sustain us
The sun and the night will come into our eyes
Without ever changing them

Our certain space our pure air is sufficient
To overcome the delay ingrained by habit
We shall all approach a new memory
Together we shall speak a sentient language.

*

Oh my contrary brothers
Where did I lose you
Your eyes filled with the horrors of night
Hands heavy in the slough of early deeds
With so little hope that death is right
Oh my lost brothers

Cours Naturel [1938]

Moi je vais vers la vie j'ai l'apparence d'homme
Pour prouver que le monde est fait à ma mesure

Et je ne suis pas seul
Mille images de moi multiplient ma lumière
Mille regards pareils égalisent la chair
C'est l'oiseau c'est l'enfant c'est le roc c'est la plaine
Qui se mêlent à nous
L'or éclate de rire de se voir hors du gouffre
L'eau le feu se dénudent pour une seule saison
Il n'y a plus d'éclipse au front de l'univers

*

Mains par nos mains reconnues
Lèvres à nos lèvres confondues
Les premières chaleurs florales
Alliées à la fraicheur du sang
Le prisme respire avec nous
Aube abondante
Au sommet de chaque herbe reine
Au sommet des mousses à la pointe des neiges
Des vagues des sables bouleversés
Des enfances persistantes
Hors de toutes les cavernes
Hors de nous-mêmes.

The Natural Course [1938]

As I turn toward life I look like a man
To prove the world is made to my size

And I am not alone
A thousand images of me multiply my light
A thousand like glances equalize this flesh
The bird the child the rock and the plain
Are as one with our lives
Gold bursts out laughing to find itself out of the pit
Water and fire are laid bare for a single season
The brow of the universe is no longer darkened by an eclipse

*

Hands clasped in recognition
Lips touching
First warm days of early blooms
Allied to the stirring of blood
The prism breathes with us
Abundant dawn
At the tip of each queenly blade of grass
At the tip of mosses and snow-flecked
Of waves of tumbled sands
Of enduring childhood
Outside all the caverns
Outside ourselves.

NOVEMBRE 1936

Regardez travailler les bâtisseurs de ruines
Ils sont riches patients ordonnés noirs et bêtes
Mais ils font de leur mieux pour être seuls sur terre
Ils sont au bord de l'homme et le comblent d'ordures
Ils plient au ras du sol des palais sans cervelle.

On s'habitue à tout
Sauf à ces oiseaux de plomb
Sauf à leur haine de ce qui brille
Sauf à leur céder la place.

Parlez du ciel le ciel se vide
L'automne nous importe peu
Nos maîtres ont tapé du pied
Nous avons oublié l'automne
Et nous oublierons nos maîtres.

Ville en baisse océan fait d'une goutte d'eau sauvée
D'un seul diamant cultivé au grand jour
Madrid ville habituelle à ceux qui ont souffert
De cet épouvantable bien qui nie être en exemple
Qui ont souffert
De la misère indispensable à l'éclat de ce bien.

Que la bouche remonte vers sa vérité
Souffle rare sourire comme une chaîne brisée
Que l'homme délivré de son passé absurde
Dresse devant son frère un visage semblable

Et donne à la raison des ailes vagabondes.

The Natural Course [1938]

NOVEMBER 1936

See the builders of ruins at work
They are rich patient orderly mean and stupid
But they are doing their best to be alone on earth
They are heaping filth on humankind
Mindless they crush palates[1] to the ground.

We get used to anything
Except these leaden birds[2]
Except their hatred for whatever shines
Except giving them our rightful place.

Speak of the sky and the sky empties
Autumn means little to us
Our masters have tapped their feet
We have forgotten autumn
We shall forget our masters.

City at ebb tide ocean made of a drop of water saved
Of a single diamond cultivated in daylight
Madrid city familiar to those who have suffered
From this frightful claim denies it's an example
For those who have suffered from the misery
Essential to its claims.

Let the mouth return to its truth
Precious breath a smile like a broken chain
Let man delivered of his absurd past
Raise a similar countenance to his brother

And lend roving wings to reason.

---

[1] *les palais*, in French, means palaces or palates; when brains are blown
out, the second interpretation is accurate. [2] Bombers attacking Spanish
cities at the beginning of the Spanish Civil War. When the Nazis bombed
Guernica in broad daylight, on market day, more than 2000 were killed.

Cours Naturel [1938]

COEUR À PIC

Le torrent son petit tonnerre
La forêt aux îles plus belles
Que les ailes des paradis
Les lampes éteintes des mares
Les mousses la nouvelle neige
Les joncs cambrés aux regards lisses
Les parfums des champs par bouffées
Le pain la poitrine en avant

Les nids ravagés des armoires
Les guenilles pâles du lit
Les palisades d'un piano
Qui n'est pas là depuis longtemps
Ma plume ce soutien débile
Le langage des fleurs du mur
Le portrait de Nusch sur la table
Imposant rythme couleurs santé
Aux cloches sourdes des paupières

Animaux sous le fouet volant
Du cirque qui gonfle ses toiles
Villages bien peuplés eau pleine
Air teinté d'ombres d'astres d'hommes
Feux des marins et des bergers
Rues et maisons tendues de feux
Lampes de pain enfants de feuilles
Pain des enfants parfum des femmes
Moulins des miroirs et des yeux

Iles des seins sillons des mots
Neige câline de la force
Mares fanées de la fatigue
Torrents d'animaux lourds de sang
Travail secret miel noir des songes
Trésors noués par des désastres
Sang commun sur toute la terre.

PRECIPITOUS HEART

The rushing stream its little thunder
The forest with its islands
More beautiful than wings of paradise
Extinguished lamps of ponds
Mosses and new snow
March reeds leaning with limpid gaze
Whiffs of perfumes from the fields
Loaves of bread puffed up with pride

Ravaged nests of closets
Pale tattered bed clothes
Palisades of a piano
That hasn't been there long
My pen this infirm support
The language of wall flowers
The portrait of Nusch on the table
Anointing the mute bells of my eyelids
With rhythm colors and health

Animals under the flying whiplash
Of the circus blowing up its canvases
Well populated villages full waters
Air tinted with shadows stars and men
The fires of sailors and shepherds
Streets and houses lit up with fires
Lamps made of bread children out of leaves
Children's bread perfume of women
Mills of mirrors and eyes

Islands of breasts words in ditches
Caressing snow of strength
Shrinking pools of fatigue
Torrents of animals heavy with blood
Secret work black honey of dreams
Treasures tied up by disasters
Common blood over the land.

Cours Naturel [1938]

LA VICTOIRE DE GUERNICA

1

Beau monde des masures
De la mine et des champs

2

Visages bons au feu visages bons au froid
Aux refus à la nuit aux injures aux coups

3

Visages bons à tout
Voici le vide qui vous fixe
Votre mort va servir d`exemple

4

La mort coeur renversé

5

Ils vous font payer le pain
Le ciel la terre l'eau le sommeil
Et la misère
De votre vie

6

Ils disaient désirer la bonne intelligence
Ils rationnaient les forts jugeaient les fous
Faisaient l'aumone partageaient un sou en deux
Ils saluaient les cadavres
Ils s'accablaient de politesses

7

Ils persévèrent ils exagèrent ils ne sont pas de notre monde

THE VICTORY OF GUERNICA[1]

1

Beautiful world of hovels
Of the mine and the fields

2

Good faces in the good faces in the cold
Refusing the night of curses and blows

3

Faces good for everything
Here is the void which stares at you
Your death will serve as an example

4

Death a heart upturned

5

They[1] make you pay for bread
For sky for earth water and sleep
And the misery
Of your life

6

They claimed to want good intelligence
They rationed the strong judged the mad
Gave alms split a penny in two
Did homage to the corpses
Outdid themselves with politeness

7

They persevere they exaggerate they are not of our world

---

[1]The Fascist leaders of Spain, Germany and Italy and those who
collaborated with them.

8

Les femmes les enfants ont le même trésor
De feuilles vertes de printemps et de lait pur
Et de durée
Dans leurs yeux purs

9

Les femmes les enfants ont le même trésor
Dans les yeux
Les hommes le défendent comme ils peuvent

10

Fes femmes les enfants ont les mêmes roses rouges
Dans les yeux
Chacun montre son sang

11

La peur et le courage de vivre et de mourir
La mort si difficile et si facile

12

Hommes pour qui ce trésor fut chanté
Hommes pour qui ce trésor fut gâché

13

Hommes réels pour qui le désespoir
Alimente le feu dévorant de l'espoir
Ouvrons ensemble le dernier bourgeon de l'avenir

14

Parias la mort la terre et la hideur
De nos ennemis ont la couleur
Monotone de notre nuit
Nous en aurons raison.

8

The women and children have the same treasure
Of the green leaves of spring and of pure milk
And long patience
In their pure eyes

9

The women and children have the same treasure
In their eyes
The men defend it as best they can

10

The women the children have the same red roses
In their eyes
Each one shows his blood

11

Fear and the courage to live and die
Death so difficult and so easy

12

Men for whom this treasure was sung
Men for whom this treasure was spoiled

13

Real men for whom despair
Feeds the devouring fire of hope
Together let us open the final budding flower of the future

14

Pariahs death earth and the horror
Of our enemies have
The monotonous color of our night
Our truth will prevail.

Cours Naturel *[1938]*

PAROLES PEINTES

Pour tout comprendre
Même
L'arbre au regard de proue
L'arbre adoré des lézards et des lianes
Même le feu même l'aveugle

Pour réunir aile et rosée
Coeur et nuage jour et nuit
Fenêtre et pays de partout

Pour abolir
La grimace du zéro
Qui demain roulera sur l'or

Pour trancher
Les petites manières
Des géants nourris d'eux-mêmes

Pour voir tous les yeux réfléchis
Par tous les yeux

Pour voir tous les yeux aussi beaux
Qu'est-ce qu'ils voient
Mer absorbante

Pour que l'on rie légèrement
D'avoir eu chaud d'avoir eu froid
D'avoir eu faim d'avoir eu soif

Pour que parler
Soit aussi généreux
Qu'embrasser

94

PAINTED WORDS

To understand it all
Even
The tree looking like a ship's prow
The tree adored by lizards and vines
Even fire even the blind

To bring together the wing and the dew
Heart and cloud day and night
Window and the land beyond

To abolish
The grimace of zero
Which tomorrow will be rolling on gold

To cut through
The petty manners
Of giants nourished on themselves

To see all eyes mirrored
In all other eyes

To see all eyes as beautiful
What do they see
Absorbent ocean

So that we may laugh lightly
At having been hot at having been cold
At having been hungry at having been thirsty

So that speaking
May be as generous
As embracing

Cours Naturel [1938]

Pour mêler baigneuse et rivière
Cristal et danseuse d'orage
Aurore et la saison des seins
Désirs et sagesse d'enfance

Pour donner à la femme
Méditative et seule
La forme des caresses
Qu'elle a rêvées

Pour que les déserts soient dans l'ombre
Au lieu d'être dans
Mon
Ombre

Donner
Mon
Bien
Donner
Mon
Droit.

To mingle bather and river
Crystal and storm-dancer
Dawn and the season of breasts
Desires and the wisdom of childhood

To give woman
Thoughtful and alone
The form of caresses
She has dreamed of

So that deserts may be in the shadow
Instead of being in
My
Shadow

To give
My
All
To give
My
Right.

Chanson complète [1938-1939]

> *Trois chevaux aigus*
> *Sauf vers le nord*
> *Trois routes perdus*
> *Sauf vers l'aurore.*

NOUS SOMMES

Tu vois le feu du soir qui sort de sa coquille
Et tu vois la forêt enfouie dans la fraîcheur

Tu vois la plaine nue aux flancs du ciel traînard
La neige haute comme la mer
Et la mer haute dans l'azur

Pierres parfaites et bois doux secours voilés
Tu vois des villes teintes de mélancolie
Dorée des trottoirs pleins d'excuses
Une place où la solitude a sa statue
Souriante et l'amour une seule maison

Tu vois les animaux
Sosies malins sacrifiés l'un à l'autre
Frères immaculés aux ombres confondues
Dans un désert de sang

Tu vois un bel enfant quand il joue quand il rit
Il est bien plus petit
Que le petit oiseau du bout des branches

Tu vois un paysage aux saveurs d'huile et d'eau
D'où la roche est exclue où la terre abandonne
Sa verdure à l'été qui la couvre de fruits

*

Complete song [1938-1939]

> *Three keen horses*
> *Except towards the north*
> *Three lost roads*
> *Except towards the dawn*

WE ARE

You see the fire of evening emerging from its shell
And the forest hidden in cool shadows

You see the bare plain flanked by the drifting sky
Snow high as the ocean
Ocean high in the azure sky

Perfect stones and soft woods veiled harbingers
You see cities imbued with melanocholy
Adorned with sidewalks full of excuses
A public square where solitude has its smiling statue
And love has a single house

You see the animals
Cunning clones sacrificed to each other
Immaculate brothers their shadows merged
In a desert of blood

You see a fine child laughing as he plays
He seems much smaller than the little bird
At the tip of the branch

You see a landscape with savors of oil and water
Where no rock is included where the land abandons
Its green to summer covering it with fruit

*

Chanson complète [1938-1939]

Des femmes descendant de leur miroir ancien
T'apportent leur jeunesse et leur foi en la tienne
Et l'une sa clarté la voile qui t'entraîne
Te fait secrètement voir le monde sans toi.

*

C'est avec nous que tout vivra

Bêtes mes vrais étendards d'or
Plaines mes bonnes aventures
Verdure utile villes sensibles
À votre tête viendront des hommes

Des hommes de dessous les sueurs les coups les larmes
Mais qui vont cueillir tous leurs songes

Je vois des hommes vrais sensibles bons utiles
Rejeter un fardeau plus mince que la mort
Et dormir de joie au bruit du soleil.

Complete song [1938-1939]

Women descending from their antique mirror
Bring you their youth and their faith in yours
One offers her vision the veil that leads you on
Secretly shows you the world without you.

*

The world will come alive with us

Beasts my true golden standards
Plains my good adventures
Useful verdure responsive cities
Men will come to guide you

Men from beneath sweat blows and tears
But who will gather all their dreams

I see good responsive men helplful and true
Casting off a burden thinner than death
And sleeping joyful in the sound of the sun.

NULLE RUPTURE:

LA LUMIÈRE ET LA CONSCIENCE
M'ACCABLENT D'AUTANT DE MYSTÈRES,
DE MISÈRES QUE LA NUIT ET LES RÊVES

Naissance de la nuit
Étoile de la rose
Secouant ses reflets
Voici dans un miroir
Qu'une lampe comme un matin d'hiver s'avance
Trébuchante
Bientôt brisée
Ayant laissé tomber sa toilette de fauve
La tempête la prend mourante au sein d'un fou
Roi des marais
Roi des brouillards
Qui chantait les vendanges d'une lune immense

Dans le four du miroir cuit le pain de la lampe
La peur de ne pouvoir conserver dans la nuit
Ce qui bouge et qui change
La peur de ne pouvoir vivre la nuit
Dans des draps éternels
Lumière propre aux rêves d'être malgré soi
Laborieux espoir de ne pas dire l'heure
Mais le temps innocent

Aveugle imaginaire sans mémoire
Le fou dans l'ombre fidèle au sang
Aux flammes d'ombre
Oeil de brouillard
Oeil de marais
Albâtre mur
Et les reflets de la chaleur
La lumière qui s'enferme

Complete song   [1938-1939]

NO BREAK:

LIGHT AND CONSCIENCE
OVERWHELM ME WITH AS MANY MYSTERIES,
AS MANY MISERIES, AS NIGHT AND DREAMS

Birth of the night
Star of the rose
Shaking its reflections
Here in a mirror
Let a lamp like a winter morning advance
Stumbling
Soon broken
Its tawny apparel cast off
The tempest takes it dying to the heart of a madman
King of the swamps
King of the mists
Who sang of harvesting an immense moon

In the oven of the mirror the lamp's bread is cooking
The fear of being unable to conserve in the night
What moves and changes
The fear of not being able to live at night
In eternal sheets
Light of dreams of being hardworking in spite of oneself
Hope of not telling the hour
Rather innocent time

Blind imaginary without memory
The madman in the shadow faithful to his blood
With shadowy flames
Eye of the fog
Eye of the swamp
Alabaster wall
And the reflections of warmth
The light which is enclosed

Chanson complète [1938-1939]

Fenêtre
Sous la peau du miroir bat le coeur de la lampe
Fenêtre
Hier encore
Des portraits
Étaient à la fenêtre
À guetter l'arrivée de la lumière reine
Fenêtre
Hier encore
Des portraits défendaient les murs de la maison
Barrant tous les chemins nocturnes du délire
Retenant le fou en proie au vertige
Parmi ses pierres

Choisir
Ou ce refuge sans couleurs
Ou le sable fin de la chute
Et le ruisseau de sang qui va s'éteindre
Et le ruisseau de nuit qui bercera sous terre
Des mains seules des yeux seuls
Le crâne comme une montagne
Que personne ne gravira

Ou ce refuge sans vertu
Qu'envoûte une lampe inutile
Cette inondation de rides de manies
De regards mornes partagés par un miroir infâme
Ces monotones pas du coeur dans l'avenir
Les peurs les doutes l'ignorance imperméable

Plus rien qu'un méchant crépuscule.

Window
Under the skin of the window beats the heart of the lamp
Window
Yesterday once again
Portraits
Were at the window
Watching for the arrival of the light queen
Window
Again yesterday
Portraits were defending the walls of the house
Barring all nocturnal paths of delirium
Holding back the madman a prey to vertigo
Among its stones

To choose
Either this dull refuge
Or the fine sand of the falls
And the blood stream which will be extinguished
And the night stream which will cradle underground
Hands alone eyes alone
The skull like a mountain
Which none will climb

Or this refuge without virtue
On which a useless lamp casts a spell
This inundation of wrinkles of manias
Of mournful glances shared by an infamous mirror
These monotonous steps of the heart into the future
Fears doubts impermeable ignorance

Nothing's left but a mean twilight.

JUSTE MILIEU

. . . .

CRÉPUSCULE

Désert vertical, le verrier creusait la terre, le fossoyeur voulait se pendre et dans la fumée de ma tête s'organisait l'oubli. C'était l'heure entre chien et loup, entre suie et poix. Un joli vertige. Avant de disparaître, le ciel fit une grimace cornue. Je vivais, petit, tranquille, bien au chaud, car j'avais enchâssé ma précieuse fureur diurne dans la dure poitrine de mes ennemis vaincus.

. . . .

INSOMNIE

Je reculais lentement. Je devins inactif, improductif; je devins intangible, invisible, incompréhensible. Une nuit encore, on m'illumina, faiblement; puis ce fut la tombe, toute panachée de racines, d'animaux luisants, d'os. Personne ne s'en doutait, personne ne m'y suivit.

. . . .

MORT

La mort vint toute seule, s'en alla toute seule et celui qui aimait la vie resta seul.

. . . .

PAUVRE

C'est le mystère de l'air pur, celui du blé. C'est le mystère de l'orage, celui du pauvre. Dans les pauvres maisons, on aime le silence . . . . Mais les enfants crient, les femmes pleurent, les hommes crient, la musique est horrible. On voudrait faire la moisson et l'on fait honte aux étoiles. Quel désordre noir, quelle pourriture, quel désastre! Jetons ces langes au ruisseau, jetons nos femmes à la rue, jetons notre pain aux ordures, jetons-nous au feu, jetons-nous au feu!

MIDWAY[1]

. . . .

TWILIGHT

A vertical desert, the glassmaker was digging in the ground, the gravedigger wanted to hang himself, and in my smoky head forgetting was settling in.

It was dusk, "the hour between dog and wolf, soot and pitch."[2] Quite a nice vertigo. Before disappearing, the sky put on a face with horns. I was quite small, living without worry, cozy and warm, for I had enshrined my precious daytime fury in my hardhearted, vanquished enemies.

. . . .

INSOMNIA

I was slowly withdrawing. I became inactive, unproductive, intangible, invisible, incomprehensible. One more night, a light shone weakly upon me; then it was the tomb, spruced up with roots, glowing animals and bones. No one suspected, none followed me there.

. . . .

DEATH

Death came alone, went away alone, and the one who loved life remained alone.   . . . .

POOR

The mystery of wheat is the mystery of pure air. It's the mystery of the storm, of the poor. In poor abodes, silence is preferred . . . . But the children cry out, women weep, men shout, the music is awful. They would like to harvest yet they shame the stars. What black disorder, what rot, what a disaster! Let's throw these diapers into the stream, our wives into the street, our bread to the garbage, let's throw ourselves into the fire!

---

[1] Between sleep and waking, the poet's dreams reveal his desires and fears, of inadequacy or death, or of the hunger and frustrations of the poor.

[2] At dusk we can't distinguish between dog and wolf, or soot and black pitch.

> *Voir, c'est comprendre, juger, transformer,*
> *imaginer, oublier ou s'oublier, être ou disparaître.*

À PABLO PICASSO

I

Les uns ont inventé l'ennui d'autres le rire
Certains taillent à la vie un manteau d'orage
Ils assomment les papillons font tourner les oiseaux en eau
Et s'en vont mourir dans le noir

Toi tu as ouvert des yeux qui vont leur voie
Parmi les choses naturelles à tous les ages
Tu a fait la moisson des choses naturelles
Et tu sèmes pour tous les temps

On te prêchait l'âme et le corps
Tu as remis la tête sur le corps
Tu as percé la langue de l'homme rassasié
Tu as brûlé le pain bénit de la beauté
Un seul coeur anima l'idole et les esclaves
Et parmi tes victimes tu continues à travailler
Innocemment

C'en est fini des joies greffées sur le chagrin.

II

Un bol d'air bouclier de lumière

Derrière ton regard aux trois épées croisées
Tes cheveux nattent le vent rebelle
Sous ton teint renversé la coupole et la hache de ton front
Délivrent la bouche tendue à nu
Ton nez est rond et calme
Tes sourcils sont légers l'oreille est transparente

À ta vue je sais que rien n'est perdu.

Let others see   [1938-1939]

> *Seeing is understanding, judging, transforming, imagining,*
> *forgetting or forgetting oneself, being or disappearing.*

TO PABLO PICASSO

I

Some invented boredom others laughter
Still others fit storm coats to their lives
They bash butterflies reduce birds to water
Then go off to die in the dark

You have opened eyes that make their way
Among natural things at all ages
You have harvested natural things
You sow for all seasons

They preached body and soul to you
You put the head back on the body
You pierced the tongue of the satiated
You burned the blessed bread of beauty
A single heart animated the idol and the slaves
And among your victims you continue to labor
Innocently

Finished are joys grafted onto sorrows.

II

A bowl of air a shield of light

Behind your gaze of three crossed swords
Your hair braids the rebellious wind
Under your inverted color the cupola and axe of your brow
Deliver your wide bared mouth
Your nose is round and calm
Your eyebrows are light your ear transparent

Seeing you I know that nothing has been lost.

III

Fini d'errer tout est possible
Puisque la table est droite comme un chêne
Couleur de bure couleur d'espoir
Puisque dans notre champ petit comme un diamant
Tient le reflet de toutes les étoiles

Tout est possible on est ami avec l'homme et la bête
À la façon d'arc-en-ciel

Tour à tour brulante et glaciale
Notre volonté est de nacre
Elle change de bourgeons et de fleurs non selon l'heure mais selon
La main et l'oeil que nous nous ignorions

Nous toucherons tout ce que nous voyons
Aussi bien le ciel que la femme
Nous joignons nos mains à nos yeux
La fête est nouvelle.

IV

L'oreille du taureau à la fenêtre
De la maison sauvage où le soleil blessé
Un soleil d'intérieur se terre

Tentures du réveil les parois de la chambre
Ont vaincu le sommeil.

Let others see [1938-1939]

III

Our wanderings are over anything is possible
Since the table is straight as an oak
The color of homespun the color of hope
Since our field small as a diamond
Holds the reflection of all the stars

Anything is possible we are friends of man and beast
In the manner of a rainbow

In turn burning and glacial
Our will is of mother-of-pearl
Changing buds and blossoms not by the hour but according to
The hand and eye we did not know in ourselves

We will touch all we see
The sky as well as the woman
We bring our hands to our eyes
It's a new celebration.

IV

The bull's ear at the window
Of the wild house where the wounded sun
An interior sun is brought down[1]

Tapestries of awakening the bedroom walls
Have overcome sleep.

---

[1] Reference to one of Picasso's drawings. The bull and horse appear in his drawings of bullfights, and in scenes of the Spanish Civil War, such as his series of etchings "The dream and lie of Franco".

V

Est-il argile plus aride que tous ces journaux déchirés
Avec lesquels tu te lanças à la conquête de l'aurore
De l'aurore d'un humble objet
Tu dessines avec amour ce qui attendait d'exister
Tu dessines dans le vide
Comme on ne dessine pas
Généreusement tu découpas la forme d'un poulet
Tes mains jouèrent avec ton paquet de tabac
Avec un verre avec un litre qui gagnèrent

Le monde enfant sortit d'un songe

Bon vent pour la guitare et pour l'oiseau
Une seule passion pour le lit et la barque
Pour la verdure neuve et pour le vin nouveau

Les jambes des baigneuses dénudent vague et plage
Matin tes volets bleus se ferment sur la nuit
Dans les sillons la caille a l'odeur de noisette
Des vieux mois d'août et des jeudis
Récoltes bariolées paysannes sonores
Écailles des marais sécheresse des nids

Visage aux hirondelles amères au chouchant rauque

Le matin allume un fruit vert
Dore les blés les joues les coeurs
Tu tiens la flamme entre tes doigts
Et tu peins comme un incendie

Enfin la flamme unit enfin la flamme sauve.

112

V

Is there clay drier than all these torn newspapers
With which you set out to conquer the dawn
The dawn of a humble object [1]
You draw lovingly what was waiting to exist
You draw in space
Like nobody else
Generously you cut out the form of a chicken
Your hands played with your tobacco pouch
With a glass a bottle winners both

The world like a child came out of a dream

Fair weather for the guitar and for the bird
A single passion for the bed and the boat
For spring green and new wine

Bathers' legs denude the waves and beach
At dawn your blue shutters close upon the night
In the furrows the quail with its scent of hazelnuts
Of August months gone by and Thursdays
Mottled harvests resounding peasants
Scales of swamps aridity of nests

Face of bitter swallows at the raucous sunset

Morning kindles a green fruit
Gilds wheatfields cheeks and hearts
You hold the flame between your fingers
You paint like a conflagration

At last the flame unites the flame saves

---

[1] Refers to Picasso's collages cut out of newspapers, creating guitars,
vases on tables, etc. in the Cubist style of Georges Braque or Juan Gris.

VI

Je reconnais l'image variable de la femme
Astre double miroir mouvant
La négatrice du désert et de l'oubli
Source aux seins de bruyère étincelle confiance
Donnant le jour au jour et son sang au sang
Je t'entends chanter sa chanson
Ses mille formes imaginaires
Ses couleurs qui préparent le lit de la campagne
Puis qui s'en vont teinter des mirages nocturnes

Et quand la caresse s'enfuit
Reste l'immense violence
Reste l'injure aux ailes lasses
Sombre métamorphose un peuple solitaire
Que le malheur dévore

Drame de voir où il n'y a rien à voir
Que soi et ce qui est semblable à soi

Tu ne peux pas t'anéantir
Tout renaît sous tes yeux justes

Et sur les fondations des souvenirs présents
Sans ordre ni désordre avec simplicité
S'élève le prestige de donner à voir.

VI

I recognize the changing image of woman
Double star moving mirror
Negation of the desert and forgetting
Wellspring with breasts of heather sparks confidence
Giving light back to the day and her blood to life's blood
I hear you singing her song
Her thousand forms imagined
Her colors that prepare the bed of the field
Then go on to color nocturnal mirages

And when the caress flees
Great violence remains
The insult with tired wings
Somber metamorphosis a lonely people
Devoured by misfortune

The drama of seeing where there's nothing to see
But yourself and what resembles you

You cannot reduce yourself to nothing
All is reborn under your just eyes

And on the foundations of present memories
Without order or disorder with simplicity
Rises the marvelous power to help others to see.

VIVRE

Nous avons tous deux nos mains à donner
Prenez ma main je vous conduirai loin

J'ai vécu plusieurs fois mon visage a changé
À chaque seuil à chaque main que j'ai franchis
Le printemps familial renaissait
Gardant pour lui pour moi sa neige périssable
La mort et la promise
La future aux cinq doigts serrés et relâchés

Mon âge m'accordait toujours
De nouvelles raisons de vivre par autrui
Et d'avoir en mon coeur le sang d'un autre coeur

Ah le garçon lucide que je fus et que je suis
Devant la blancheur des faibles filles aveugles
Plus belles que la lune blonde fine usée
Par le reflet des chemins de la vie
Chemin des mousses et des arbres
Du brouillard et de la rosée
Du jeune corps qui ne monte pas seul
À sa place sur terre
Le vent le froid la pluie le bercent
L'été en fait un homme

Présence ma vertu dans chaque main visible
La seule mort c'est solitude
De délice en furie de furie en clarté
Je me construis entier à travers tous les êtres
À travers tous les temps au sol et dans les nues.

TO LIVE

We both have our hands to give
Take mine I shall lead you afar

I have lived several times my face has changed
With every threshold I have crossed and every hand clasped
Familial springtime was reborn
Keeping for itself and for me its perishable snow
Death and the betrothed
The future with five fingers clenched and letting go

My age always gave me
New reasons for living through others
For having the blood of another's heart in mine

Oh the lucid fellow I was and that I am
Before the pallor of frail blind girls
Lovelier than the delicate worn moon so fair
By the reflection of life's ways
A trail of moss and trees
Of mist and morning dew
Of the young body which does not rise alone
To its place on earth
Wind cold and rain cradle it
Summer makes a man of it

Presence is my virtue in each visible hand
Only death is solitude
From delight to fury from fury to clarity
I make myself whole through all beings
Through all weather on the earth and in the clouds

Le livre ouvert I [1938-1940]

Saisons passantes je suis jeune
Et fort à force d'avoir vécu
Je suis jeune et mon sang s'élève sur mes ruines

Nous avons nos mains à mêler
Rien jamais ne peut mieux séduire
Que notre attachement l'un à l'autre forêt
Rendant la terre au ciel et le ciel à la nuit

À la nuit qui prépare un jour interminable.

JUSTICE

Lourde image d'argent misère aux bras utiles
À l'ancienne à la simple on mangera les fleurs
Ceux qui pleurent de peine auront les yeux crevés
Et ceux qui rient d'horreur seront récompensés.

ENFANTS

L'alouette et le hibou dans le même jardin
Étoilé d'oeufs brisés par des becs et des ailes
Les agneaux et des loups dans les mêmes beaux draps
Dans le lait débordant de leur gloutonnerie.

Through the passing seasons I am young
And strong for having lived
I am young my blood rises over my ruins

We have our hands to entwine
Nothing can ever seduce better
Than our bonding to each other a forest
Returning earth to sky and the sky to night

To the night which prepares an unending day.

JUSTICE

Heavy silver image misery with useful arms
In the old way simply we shall eat flowers
Those who weep from suffering shall have their eyes bashed in
And those who laugh in horror shall be rewarded.

CHILDREN

Skylark and owl in the same garden
Starred with eggs shattered by beaks and wings
Lambs and wolves in the same fine sheets
In the overflowing milk of their gluttony.

QUATRE DEUILS

I

Pain ronronnant banale tentation

Ordinaire larron pauvre homme
Entame ton action idéale si simple
Réduire ton désir
Entame sans détours élégants ton bien

Ton or ce pain
Un sou des autres
Les espoirs sacrifiés périmés atrophiés sans coeur
Yeux sans un nerf front bas

Inepte sourires saufs serpents réchauffés
Eclairs zézéyants vagissant élans manqués
Ordure ce pain
Un sou à perdre.

II

Ravir sans honte nids et fruits

Sauvage à table
Simule un repas indécent
Et que ton rire verse vrai
L'éclat du soleil sous les feuilles

Allons toujours un geste en plus
Une aile en plus pour les oiseaux
Une prune pour les guêpes
Et toujours un mot pour rien

Open book I [1938-1940]

FOUR BEREAVEMENTS

I

Bread purring banal temptation

Common thief poor man
Undertake your simple ideal act
Reduce your desire
Undertake well-being without elegant detours

Your gold this bread
A penny from others
Hopes sacrificed overdue atrophied heartless
Listless gaze lowered brow

Awkward smiles except for rewarmed snakes
Lightning flashing squeaking failed efforts
Garbage bread
A penny to lose.

II

Shamelessly robbing nests and fruits

Uncouth at the table
Make believe an indecent meal
And may your laughter pour forth in truth
Sparkling sunshine beneath the foliage

Let's move along always one more gesture
One more wing for the birds
A plum for the wasps
And always a word that costs nothing

Bonne terre changée en homme
Attention tu ne sais pas vivre
Errant couvre avec soin tes traces
Pour ne pas disparaître

III

Je tremble c'est des misères misère
La fin viendra en moment inutile
Le soleil prend sa place sur la terre
Mais ce n'est plus sur lui que je m'appuie

Que mon corps gèle et que mon coeur durcisse
Il me faut bien trouver le lieu secret
Où j'oublierai lentement que j'existe
Alors mes frères n'ayant plus de frère

Ne craindront plus l'image de leur mort.

IV

Meurt-de-faim mendiants et larrons
Votre chemin a la largeur
Du monde et vous vous égarez
Et vous crevez dans les prisons

Vous ne savez rien que manger
Et manger vous est aventure
Vous faites valoir le bonheur
Pour n'en recevoir que souillure

Vous supportez toute souffrance
Pourvu qu'elle soit imprévue
Et l'on vous montre l'âpre horreur
De votre vie réglée d'avance

Good earth changed into a man
Watch out you don't know how to live
Wandering cover your footprints carefully
So you don't disappear

III

I tremble it's the misery of miseries
The end will come at an idle moment
The sun takes its place in the land
But I depend on it no longer

Let my body freeze and my heart harden
I must find the secret place
Where I will forget gradually that I exist
Leaving my brothers without a brother

No longer will they fear the image of their death.

IV

Dying-of-hunger beggars and thieves
Your path is as wide as the world
And you stray from the path
And you die in the prisons

You know only about eating
And eating is an adventure for you
You give value to happiness
Only to be spat upon

You put up with all the suffering
As long as it's unexpected
And they show you the raw horror
Of your life ordered from the start

ONZE POÈMES DE PERSISTANCE

RIEN QUE LE GRAND AIR

Au tombeau des couleurs
Dont les vitres faiblissent
La fumée s'évanouit.

LE ROLE DE L'IMPUISSANCE

Des larmes ont lavé ce visage rieur
Qui amadoue un enfant dur aux yeux hautains.

JOURS SANS OMBRES

Ses seins ses yeux ses mains ensemble
Unissent les jours les plus beaux.

BARIOLAGE

Caresse lueur sous la cendre
Violette sous des roses blanches.

PREMIER MOMENT

Entre mon lit sombre et l'écume ardente
Du jour révélateur
S'inscrit une irritante loi bouger.

ELEVEN POEMS OF PERSISTENCE

ONLY THE OPEN AIR

At the tomb of colors
Whose window panes grow dim
Smoke vanishes.

THE ROLE OF HELPLESSNESS

Tears have washed this laughing countenance
That coaxes a resistant child with defiant eyes.

DAYS WITHOUT SHADOWS

Her breasts and eyes and hands together
Integrate the finest days.

MEDLEY

Caress glowing under the cinders
Violet under white roses.

FIRST MOMENT

Between my dark bed and the burning foam
Of revealing day is inscribed
An irritating law to get moving.

LES DIEUX

Géant rouge géant blanc
Le vin le pain
Cultivent les hommes.

L'ORAGE

Mon chien s'inquiète d'un miroir
Son front se ride au moindre bruit
Le vent mange des ailes.

PROPORTIONS

Si le ciel vide s'agrandissait
Cet arbre solitaire
Disparaitrait.

PREMIER ET DERNIER ACTE DE LA TRAGÉDIE

Et contre ma folie donne-moi ton amour
Contre mon sang versé ton coeur
Ce soir nous jouons sans public.

RENONCEMENT

Or une rivière s'allongea
Pour ne pas se perdre.

INDÉPASSABLE

Aucune cible ne dissipe
Le voyageur percé de flèches
Le voyageur infatigable.

THE GODS

Red giant white giant
Wine and bread
Cultivate people.

STORM

My dog is worried by a mirror
His brow is wrinkled by the slightest sound
The wind is eating wings.

PROPORTIONS

If the empty sky got any bigger
That solitary tree
Would disappear.

FIRST AND LAST ACT OF THE TRAGEDY

To cure my madness give me your love
For my spilt blood your heart
This evening we play without an audience.

DENIAL

So a river got longer
To avoid getting lost.

UNPASSABLE

No target dissipates
The traveller pierced by arrows
The tireless traveler.

Le livre ouvert I [1938-1940]

POUR VIVRE ICI

I

Je fis un feu, l'azur m'ayant abandonné,
Un feu pour être son ami
Un feu pour m'introduire dans la nuit d'hiver,
Un feu pour vivre mieux.

Je lui donnai ce que le jour m'avait donné:
Les forêts, les buissons, les champs de blé, les vignes
Les nids et leurs oiseaux, les maisons et leurs clés,
Les insectes, les fleurs, les fourrures, les fêtes.

Je vécus au seul bruit des flammes crépitantes,
Au seul parfum de leur chaleur;
J'étais comme un bateau coulant dans l'eau fermée,
Comme un mort je n'avais qu'un unique élément.

II

Le mur de la fenêtre saigne
La nuit ne quitte plus ma chambre
Mes yeux pourraient voir dans le noir
S'ils ne se heurtaient à des ruines

Le seul espace libre est au fond de mon coeur
Est-ce l'espace intime de la mort
Ou celui de ma fuite

Une aile retirée blessée l'a parcouru
Par ma faiblesse tout entier il est cerné
Durerai-je prendrai-je l'aube
Je n'ai à perdre qu'un seul jour
Pour ne plus même voir la nuit

La nuit ne s'ouvre que sur moi
Je suis le rivage et la clé
De la vie incertaine.

TO LIVE HERE

I

I made a fire, the blue having abandoned me,
A fire to be its friend,
A fire to lure me into the winter night,
A fire to live a little better.

I gave it what the day had given me:
Forests, shrubs, wheat fields, vines,
Nests and their birds, houses and their keys,
Insects, flowers, furs, festivities.

I lived by the sound of the crackling flames,
By the aroma of their heat;
I was like a boat floating in still waters,
Like the dead I had but one element.

II

The windowed wall bleeds
Night no longer leaves my room
My eyes could see in the dark
If they didn't collide with ruins

The only free space is deep in my heart
Is it the intimate space of death
Or of my flight

A wounded wing withdrawn has run that course
It is completely encircled by my weakness
Will I endure to engage another dawn
I have but a single day to lose
Not even to see another night

Night opens only for me
I am the shore and the key
Of uncertain life.

III

La lune enfouie les coqs grattent leur crête
Une goutte de feu se pose sur l'eau froide
Et chante le dernier cantique de la brume

Pour mieux voir la terre
Deux arbres de feu emplissent mes yeux

Les dernières larmes dispersées
Deux arbres de feu me rendent la vie

Deux arbres nus
Nu le cri que je pousse
Terre

Terre vivante dans mon coeur
Toute distance conjurée
Le nouveau rythme de moi-même
Perpétuel

Froid plein d'ardeur froid plein d'étoiles
Et l'automne éphémère et le froid consumé
Le printemps dévoué premier reflet du temps
L'été de grâce par le coeur héros sans ombres

Je suis sur terre et tout s'accommode du feu.

. . . .

III

The moon is hidden the cocks scratch their crests
A drop of fire settles on cold water
And sings the last canticle of fog

To see the earth better
Two trees of fire fill my eyes

My last tears dispersed
Two trees of fire return my life to me

Two bare trees
Naked the cry I utter
Earth

Living earth in my heart
All distance exorcized
My new rhythm
Perpetual

Cold full of passion cold full of stars
And ephemeral autumn and the cold consumed
Devoted spring first reflection of the seasons
Summer of heartfelt grace a hero without shadows

I am of this world everything makes good use of fire.
. . . .

V

Aucun homme n'est invisible
Aucun homme n'est plus oublié en lui-meme
Aucune ombre n'est transparente

Je vois des hommes là où il n'y a que moi
Mes soucis sont brisés par des rires légers
J'entends des mots très doux croiser ma voix sérieuse
Mes yeux soutiennent un réseau de regards purs

Nous passons la montagne et la mer difficiles
Les arbres fous s'opposent à ma main jurée
Les animaux errants m'offrent leur vie en miettes
Qu'importe mon image s'est multipliée
Qu'importe la nature et ses miroirs voilés
Qu'importe le ciel vide je ne suis pas seul.

V

No man is invisible
No man is forgotten within himself
No shadow is transparent

I see others where there's only me
My cares are broken by light laughter
I hear gentle words crossing my serious voice
My eyes sustain a network of pure glances

We go beyond the forbidding mountain and ocean
Crazed trees oppose my sworn intent
Wild animals offer me their life in crumbs
What does it matter my image has multiplied
What matters nature and its veiled mirrors
What matters the empty sky for I am not alone.

Marc Chagall. Man and wolf. Lithograph. Illustration for
Le Dur désir de durer, 1950 edition. Coll. Musée Saint Denis.

III

1940 - 1944

LE TEMPS DE LA RESISTANCE

THE TIME OF THE RESISTANCE

AUSSI BAS QUE LE SILENCE

Aussi bas que le silence
D'un mort planté dans la terre
Rien que ténèbres en tête

Aussi monotone et sourd
Que l'automne dans la mare
Couverte de honte mate

Le poison veuf de sa fleur
Et de ses bêtes dorées
Crache sa nuit sur les hommes.

PATIENCE

Toi ma patiente ma patience ma parente
Gorge haut suspendue orgue de la nuit lente
Révérence cachant tous les ciels dans sa grâce
Prépare à la vengeance un lit d'où je naîtrai.

On the lower slopes [1941]

AS LOW AS SILENCE

As low as the silence
Of a dead man planted in the ground
Nothing but shadows in the head

As monotonous and muffled
As autumn in the pool
Covered with dull shame

The poison a widower of its flower
And its golden beasts
Spits out its night over men.

PATIENCE

You my patient woman my patience my parent
Throat high suspended organ of the slow night
Reverence hiding all skies in its grace
Prepare for vengeance a bed from which I shall be born.

LA HALTE DES HEURES

Immenses mots dits doucement
Grand soleil les volets fermés
Un grand navire au fil de l'eau
Ses voiles partageant le vent

Bouche bien faite pour cacher
Une autre bouche et le serment
De ne rien dire qu'à deux voix
Du secret qui raye la nuit

Le seul rêve des innocents
Un seul murmure un seul matin
Et les saisons à l'unisson
Colorant de neige et de feu

Une foule enfin réunie.

On the lower slopes [1941]

STOPPING THE HOURS

Big words spoken softly
Strong sun the shutters closed
A great ship moving with the current
Its sails sharing the wind

Mouth well made to hide
Another mouth and the pledge
To speak only with two voices
Of the secret that streaks the night

The single dream of the innocent
A single murmur a single morning
And the seasons together
Coloring with snow and fire

A multitude at last united.

LE DROIT LE DEVOIR DE VIVRE

Il n'y aurait rien
Pas un insecte bourdonnant
Pas une feuille frissonnante
Pas un animal léchant ou hurlant
Rien de chaud rien de fleuri
Rien de givre rien de brillant rien d'odorant
Pas une ombre léchée par la fleur de l'été
Pas un arbre portant des fourrures de neige
Pas une joue fardée par un baiser joyeux
Pas une aile prudente ou hardie dans le vent
Pas un coin de chair fine pas un bras chantant
Rien de libre ni de gagner ni de gâcher
Ni de s'éparpiller ni de se réunir
Pour le bien pour le mal
Pas une nuit armée d'amour ou de repos
Pas une voix d'aplomb pas une bouche émue
Pas un sein dévoilé pas une main ouverte
Pas de misére et pas de satiété
Rien d'opaque rien de visible
Rien de lourd rien de léger
Rien de mortel rien d'éternel

Il y aurait un homme
N'importe quel homme
Moi ou un autre
Sinon il n'y aurait rien.

THE RIGHT THE DUTY TO LIVE

There would be nothing
Not a buzzing insect
Not a quivering leaf
Not a creature lapping or howling
Nothing warm nothing blooming
Nothing frosted nothing shining or sweet smelling
Not a shadow licked up by a summer flower
Not a tree wearing furs of snow
No cheek blushing from a joyous kiss
No prudent or bold wing in the wind
No corner of delicate flesh nor melodious arm
Nothing free to be won or spoiled
To be scattered or gathered up
For better or for worse
No night armed with love or rest
No assured voice not even a trembling lip
Not a bared breast nor an open hand
No misery and no satiety
Nothing opaque nothing visible
Nothing heavy nothing light
Nothing mortal nothing eternal

There would have to be somebody
Anybody
Myself or another
Otherwise there would be nothing.

La dernière nuit *[1942]*

LA DERNIÈRE NUIT

I

Ce petit monde meurtrier
Est orienté vers l'innocent
Lui ôte le pain de la bouche
Et donne sa maison au feu
Lui prend sa veste et ses souliers
Lui prend son temps et ses enfants

Ce petit monde meurtrier
Confond les morts et les vivants
Blanchit la boue gracie les traîtres
Transforme la parole en bruit

Merci minuit douze fusils

II

Le prodige serait une légère poussée contre le mur
Ce serait de pouvoir secouer cette poussière

Ce serait d'être unis.

III

Ils avaient mis à vif ses mains courbé son dos
Ils avaient creusé un trou dans sa tête
Et pour mourir il avait dû souffrir
Toute sa vie

The last night [1942]

THE LAST NIGHT

I

This murderous little world
Is turned toward the innocent
Takes the bread from his mouth
Sets fire to his house
Takes his coat and shoes
Takes his time and his children

This murderous little world
Confounds the dead and the living
Whitens the mud pardons the traitors
Turns words into noise

Thanks to midnight a dozen guns

II

The wonder would be a light push against the wall
To be able to shake off this dust

It would be to be united.

III

They had skinned his hands bent his back
They had dug a hole in his head
And to die he had had to suffer
All his life

La dernière nuit [1942]

IV

Beauté créée pour les heureux
Beauté tu cours un grand danger

Ces mains croisées sur tes genoux
Sont les outils d'un assassin

Cette bouche chantant très haut
Sert de sébile au mendiant

Et cette coupe de lait pur
Devient le sein d'une putain.

V

Les pauvres ramassaient leur pain dans le ruisseau
Leur regard couvrait la lumière
Et ils n'avaient plus peur la nuit
Très faibles leur faiblesse les faisait sourire
Dans le fond de leur ombre ils emportaient leur corps
Ils ne se voyaient plus qu'à travers leur détresse
Ils ne se servaient plus que d'un langage intime
Et j'entendais parler doucement prudemment
D'un ancien espoir grand comme la main

J'entendais calculer
Les dimensions multipliées de la feuille d'automne
La fonte de la vague au sein de la mer calme
J'entendais calculer
Les dimensions multipliées de la force future.

The last night [1942]

IV

Beauty created for the happy
Beauty you run a great risk

The hands crossed on your knees
Are the tools of an assassin

This mouth singing aloud
Serves as a beggar's bowl

And this cup of pure milk
Becomes the breast of a whore.

V

The poor picked their bread from the gutter
Their look covered up the light
No longer were they afraid at night

So weak their weakness made them smile
Into the depths of their shadow they carried their bodies
They saw themselves only through their distress
They no longer used any but an intimate language
I heard them speaking softly prudently
Of an old hope as big as a hand

I heard them calculating
The multiple dimensions of an autumn leaf
The melting of the wave on the breast of a calm sea
I heard them calculate
The multipled dimensions of the future force.

VI

Je suis né derrière une façade affreuse
J'ai mangé j'ai ri j'ai rêvé j'ai eu honte
J'ai vécu comme un ombre
Et pourtant j'ai su chanter le soleil
Le soleil entier celui qui respire
Dans chaque poitrine et dans tous les yeux
La goutte de candeur qui luit après les larmes.

VII

Nous jetons le fagot des ténèbres au feu
Nous brisons les serrures rouillées de l'injustice
Des hommes vont venir qui n`ont plus peur d'eux-mêmes
Car ils sont sùrs de tous les hommes
Car l'ennemi à figure d'homme disparaît.

The last night [1942]

VI

I was born behind a hideous facade
I have eaten laughed dreamed I've been ashamed
I have lived like a shadow
Yet I knew how to sing of the sun
The entire sun which breathes
In every breast and in all eyes
The drop of candor which sparkles after tears.

VII

We throw the faggot of shadows to the fire
We break the rusted locks of injustice
Men will come no longer afraid of themselves
For they are sure of all men
As the enemy with a man's face disappears.

LIBERTÉ

Sur mes cahiers d'écolier
Sur mon pupitre et les arbres
Sur le sable sur la neige
J'écris ton nom

Sur toutes les pages lues
Sur toutes les pages blanches
Pierre sang papier ou cendre
J'écris ton nom

Sur les images dorées
Sur les armes des guerriers
Sur la couronne des rois
J'écris ton nom

Sur la jungle et le désert
Sur les nids sur les genêts
Sur l'écho de mon enfance
J'écris ton nom

Sur les merveilles des nuits
Sur le pain blanc des journées
Sur les saisons fiancées
J'écris ton nom

Sur tous mes chiffons d'azur
Sur l'étang soleil moisi
Sur le lac lune vivante
J'écris ton nom

Sur les champs sur l'horizon
Sur les ailes des oiseaux
Et sur le moulin des ombres
J'écris ton nom

Poetry and truth   [1942]

LIBERTY

On my schoolboy's notebooks
On my desk and on the trees
On sand on snow
I write your name

On all pages read
On all blank pages
Stone blood paper or ash
I write your name

On gilded images
On the weapons of warriors
On the crowns of kings
I write your name

On jungle and desert
On nests on gorse
On the echo of my childhood
I write your name

On the wonders of nights
On the white bread of days
On the seasons betrothed
I write your name

On all my azure rags
On the pool a musty sun
On the lake a living moon
I write your name

On fields on the horizon
On the wings of birds
And on the mill of shadows
I write your name

Sur chaque bouffée d'aurore
Sur la mer sur les bateaux
Sur la montagne démente
J'écris ton nom

Sur la mousse des nuages
Sur les sueurs de l'orage
Sur la pluie épaisse et fade
J'écris ton nom

Sur les formes scintillantes
Sur les cloches des couleurs
Sur la vérité physique
J'écris ton nom

Sur les sentiers éveillés
Sur les routes déployées
Sur les places qui débordent
J'écris ton nom

Sur la lampe qui s'allume
Sur la lampe qui s'éteint
Sur mes maisons réunies
J'écris ton nom

Sur le fruit coupé en deux
Du miroir et de ma chambre
Sur mon lit coquille vide
J'écris ton nom

Sur mon chien gourmand et tendre
Sur ses oreilles dressées
Sur sa patte maladroite
J'écris ton nom

On each puff of dawn
On the sea on the ships
On the demented mountain
I write your name

On the foam of the clouds
On the sweat of the storm
On the thick dull rain
I write your name

On shimmering shapes
On the bells of colors
On physical truth
I write your name

On awakened pathways
On roads spread out
On overflowing central squares
I write your name

On the lamp that is lit
On the lamp that burns out
On my houses reunited
I write your name

On the halved fruit
Of the mirror and my room
On my bed an empty shell
I write your name

On my dog greedy and tender
On his raised ears
On his awkward paw
I write your name

Sur le tremplin de ma porte
Sur les objets familiers
Sur le flot du feu béni
J'écris ton nom

Sur toute chair accordée
Sur le front de mes amis
Sur chaque main qui se tend
J'écris ton nom

Sur la vitre des surprises
Sur les lèvres attentives
Bien au-dessus du silence
J'écris ton nom

Sur mes refuges détruites
Sur mes phares écroulés
Sur les murs de mon ennui
J'écris ton nom

Sur l'absence sans désir
Sur la solitude nue
Sur les marches de la mort
J'écris ton nom

Sur la santé revenue
Sur le risque disparu
Sur l'espoir sans souvenir
J'écris ton nom

Et par le pouvoir d'un mot
Je recommence ma vie
Je suis né pour te connaître
Pour te nommer

Liberté.

On the springboard of my door
On the familiar objects
On the sea of blessed fire
I write your name

On all flesh in tune
On the foreheads of my friends
On each outstretched hand
I write your name

On the window of surprises
On the attentive lips
Well above silence
I write your name

On my destroyed refuges
On my crumbled beacons
On the walls of my concern
I write your name

On absence without desire
On naked solitude
On the steps of death
I write your name

On health restored
On risk vanished
On hope without memories
I write your name

And by the power of a word
I begin my life again
I was born to know you
To name you

Liberty.

Poésie et vérité [1942]

COUVRE-FEU

Que voulez-vous la porte était gardée
Que voulez-vous nous étions enfermés
Que voulez-vous la rue était barrée
Que voulez-vous la ville était matée
Que voulez-vous elle était affamée
Que voulez-vous nous étions désarmés
Que voulez-vous la nuit était tombée
Que voulez-vous nous nous sommes aimés.

UN LOUP

Le jour m'étonne et la nuit me fait peur
L'été me hante et l'hiver me poursuit

Un animal sur la neige a posé
Ses pattes sur le sable ou dans la boue
Ses pattes venues de plus loin que mes pas
Sur une piste où la mort
A les empreintes de la vie.

DU DEHORS

La nuit le froid la solitude
On m'enferma soigneusement
Mais les branches cherchaient leur voie dans la prison
Autour de moi l'herbe trouva le ciel
On verrouilla le ciel
Ma prison s'écroula
Le froid vivant le froid brûlant m'eut bien en main

154

CURFEW

What did you expect the door was guarded
What did you expect we were locked in
What did you expect the street was barred
What did you expect the city was in check
What did you expect it was starving
What did you expect we were disarmed
What did you expect night had fallen
What did you expect we were in love.

A WOLF

Day astonishes me and night frightens me
Summer haunts me winter is on my trail

An animal on the snow has put
His feet on the sand or in the mud
His feet have come a longer way than mine
On a path where death
Has the footprints of life.

FROM THE OUTSIDE

The night the cold the solitude
Carefully they locked me in
But the branches were finding their way in the prison
About me the grass found the sky
They locked out the sky
My prison crumbled
The living cold the burning cold had me well in hand.

DU DEDANS

Premier commandement du vent
La pluie enveloppe le jour
Premier signal d'avoir à tendre
La voile claire de nos yeux

Au front d'une seule maison
Au flanc de la muraille
Au sein d'une serre endormie
Nous fixons un feu velouté

Dehors la terre se dégrade
Dehors la tanière des morts
S'écroule et glisse dans la boue

Une rose écorchée bleuit.

LA MAIN LE COEUR LE LION L'OISEAU

Main dominé par le coeur
Coeur dominé par le lion
Lion dominé par l'oiseau

L'oiseau qu'efface un nuage
Le lion que le désert grise
Le coeur que la mort habite
La main refermée en vain

Aucun secours tout m'échappe
Je vois ce qui disparaît
Je comprends que je n'ai rien
Et je m'imagine à peine

Entre les murs une absence
Puis l'exil dans les ténèbres
Les yeux purs la tête inerte.

FROM THE INSIDE

The wind's first commandment
Rain envelops the day
First sign that we must hoist
The clear sail of our eyes

To the brow of a single house
To the side of the wall
To the heart of a sleeping greenhouse
We start up a velvet fire

Outside the ground breaks up
Outside the den of the dead
Crumbles slides into the mud

A scorched rose turns blue

HAND HEART LION BIRD

Hand ruled by the heart
Heart ruled by the lion
Lion ruled by the bird

Bird blotted out by a cloud
Lion made giddy by the desert
Heart inhabited by death
Hand clasped in vain

There's no help everything eludes me
I see what disappears
I understand I have nothing
And I barely know myself

An absence between the walls
Then exile into the shadows
Pure eyes unmoving head.

Le lit la table *[1944]*

LES SENS

Rien sinon cette clarté
La clarté de ce matin
Qui te mènera sur terre

La clarté de ce matin
Une aiguille dans du satin
Une graine dans le noir
Oeil ouvert sur un trésor

Sous les feuilles dans tes paumes
Le jeu grisant des aumônes
Chaudes
Le grand risque des refus
Blêmes

Sur les routes du hasard
Le mur dur perdra ses pierres

La clarté de ce matin
Dévêtus de tous mes regards tes seins

Tous les parfums d'un bouquet
De la violette au jasmin
En passant par le soleil
En passant par la pensée

Le bruit de la mer le bruit des galets
La mousse et l'odeur de la fleur du bois
Le miel l'odeur du pain chaud
Duvet des oiseaux nouveaux

La clarté de ce matin
La flamme qui t'enfanta
Qui naît bleue et meurt en herbe
Premier regard premier sang

Bed and table [1944]

THE SENSES

Nothing but this clarity
This clear morning light
Will lead you to the earth

This clear morning light
A needle in satin
A seed in the dark
Eye opened on a treasure

Under the leaves in your palms
The exhilarating game
Of heady alms
The great risk of pale refusals

On the roads of chance
The hard wall will loose its stones

This morning's clear light
Your breasts bared by my glance

All the bouquet's perfumes
From violet to jasmine
Filtering through sunbeams
Passing through our thoughts

The sound of the sea the sound of pebbles
Moss and scent of the wood flower
Honey the smell of warm bread
Downy breast of fledglings

This morning's clear light
The flame that gave you life
Born blue to die young
First glance first blood

Le lit la table [1944]

Dans un champ de chair touchante
Les premiers mots du bonheur
Rafraîchissent leur ferveur
Sous des voiles de rosée

Et le ciel est sur tes lèvres.

Bed and table [1944]

In a field of flesh touching
The first words of happiness
Renew their fervor
Under veils of dew

And heaven is on your lips.

CRITIQUE DE LA POÉSIE

Le feu réveille la foret
Les troncs les coeurs les mains les feuilles
Le bonheur en un seul bouquet
Confus léger fondant sucré
C'est toute une forêt d'amis
Qui s'assemble aux fontaines vertes
Du bon soleil du bois flambant

Garcia Lorca a été mis à mort

Maison d'une seule parole
Et des lèvres unies pour vivre
Un tout petit enfant sans larmes
Dans ses prunelles d'eau perdue
La lumière de l'avenir
Goutte à goutte elle comble l'homme
Jusqu'aux paupières transparentes

Saint-Pol Roux a été mis à mort
Sa fille a été suppliciée

Ville glacée d'angles semblables
Où je rêve de fruits en fleur
Du ciel entier et de la terre
Comme à de vierges découvertes
Dans un jeu qui n'en finit pas
Pierres fanées murs sans écho
Je vous évite d'un sourire

Decour a été mis a mort.

Bed and table [1944]

CRITIQUE OF POETRY

Fire wakens the forest
Tree trunks hearts hands leaves
Happiness in a single bouquet
Confused airy melting sweetened
It's a whole forest of friends
Gathering at the green fountains
Of the good sun of the flaming wood

Garcia Lorca[1] has been put to death

House of a single word
And of lips joined for living
A little child without tears
In eyes of lost waters
The light of the future
Drop by drop fills the man
Up to his transparent eyelids

Saint-Pol Roux[2] has been put to death
His daughter has been tortured

City iced in similar angles
Where I dream of ripening fruit
Of the whole sky and earth
Like virgin discoveries
In an unending game
Faded stones walls without echo
I avoid you with a smile

Decour [3] has been put to death.

---

[1] Federico Garcia Lorca, the great poet and dramatist, killed by the Spanish militia in 1936.   [2] Saint-Pol Roux, symbolist poet, was put to death after his daughter was beaten by German troops in 1941.   [3] Jacques Decour, lycée professor, director of the review *Commune* who created the clandestine review *Les lettres françaises*, was arrested and shot in 1942.

À CELLE DONT ILS RÊVENT

Neuf cent mille prisonnier
Cinq cent mille politiques
Un million de travailleurs
Maîtresse de leur sommeil
Donne-leur des forces d'homme
Le bonheur d'être sur terre
Donne-leur dans l'ombre immense
Les lèvres d'un amour doux
Comme l'oubli des souffrances

Maîtresse de leur sommeil
Fille femme soeur et mère
Aux seins gonflés de baisers
Donne-leur notre pays
Tel qu'ils l'ont toujours chéri
Un pays fou de la vie

Un pays où le vin chante
Où les moissons ont bon coeur
Où les enfants sont malins
Où les vieillards sont plus fins
Qu'arbres à fruits blancs de fleurs
Où l'on peut parler aux femmes

Neuf cent mille prisonniers
Cinq cent mille politiques
Un million de travailleurs

Maîtresse de leur sommeil
Neige noire des nuits blanches
À travers un feu exsangue
Sainte Aube à la canne blanche
Fais-leur voir un chemin neuf
Hors de leur prison de planches

TO THE ONE THEY DREAM OF

Nine hundred thousand prisoners of war
Five hundred thousand political prisoners
One million forced workers
Mistress of their slumber
Give them the strength of men
The happiness of being on earth
In the immense shadow give them
The lips of a sweet love
Like the oblivion of suffering

Mistress of their slumber
Daughter wife sister and mother
Her breasts swollen with kisses
Give them our country
As they have always loved it
A country made for life

A country where wine sings
Where harvests are good hearted
Where children are clever
Where old men are finer
Than fruit trees white with blossoms
Where one may talk to women

Nine hundred thousand prisoners of war
Five hundred thousand political prisoners
One million forced workers

Mistress of their sleep
Black snow of white sleepless nights
Across a bloodless fire
Sainte Aube with the white cane
Show them a new way
Out of their wooden prisons

Les armes de la douleur [1944]

Ils sont payés pour connaître
Les pires forces du mal
Pourtant ils ont tenu bon

Ils sont criblés de vertus
Tout autant que de blessures
Car il faut qu'ils se survivent

Maîtresse de leur repos
Maîtresse de leur éveil
Donne-leur la liberté
Mais garde-nous notre honte
D'avoir pu croire à la honte
Même pour l'anéantir.

The weapons of sorrow   [1944]

They are paid to know
The worst forces of evil
Still they have held firm

They are as riddled with virtues
As with wounds
For they must survive

Mistress of their repose
Mistress of their awakening
Give them liberty
But keep for us our shame
For having been able to believe in shame
Even to destroy it.

COURAGE

Paris a froid Paris a faim
Paris ne mange plus de marrons dans la rue
Paris a mis de vieux vêtements de vieille
Paris dort tout debout sans air dans le métro
Plus de malheur encore est imposée aux pauvres
Et la sagesse et la folie
De Paris malheureux
C'est l'air pur c'est le feu
C'est la beauté c'est la bonté
De ses travailleurs affamés
Ne crie pas au secours Paris
Tu es vivant d'une vie sans égale
Et derriére la nudité
De ta pâleur de ta maigreur
Tout ce qui est humain se révèle en tes yeux
Paris ma belle ville
Fine comme une aiguille forte comme une épée
Ingénue et savante
Tu ne supportes pas l'injustice
Pour toi c'est le seul désordre
Tu vas te libérer Paris
Paris tremblant comme une étoile
Notre espoir survivant
Tu vas te libérer de la fatigue et de la boue
Frères ayons du courage
Nous qui ne sommes pas casqués
Ni bottés ni gantés ni bien élevés
Un rayon s'allume en nos veines
Notre lumiére nous revient
Les meilleurs d'entre nous sont morts pour nous
Et voici que leur sang retrouve notre coeur

COURAGE

Paris is cold Paris is hungry
Paris no longer eats chestnuts in the street
Paris has put on its old woman's clothes
Paris sleeps standing without air in the metro
Still more suffering is imposed on the poor
And the wisdom and the folly
Of unhappy Paris
Is the pure air the fire
The beauty the goodness
Of its starving workers
Do not cry help Paris
You are alive with a life unequalled
And behind the nakedness
Of your pallor of your lean bodies
All that is human is revealed in your eyes
Paris my beautiful city
Fine as a needle strong as a sword
Simple and knowing
You do not tolerate the injustice
For you it is the sole disorder
You will free yourself Paris
Paris trembling like a star
Our surviving hope
You will free yourself from fatigue and the mire
Brothers be brave
We who do not wear helmets
Nor boots nor gloves nor good manners
A ray of light in our veins
Our light returns to us
The best among us have died for us
And now their blood finds our hearts again

Les armes de la douleur *[1944]*

Et c'est de nouveau le matin un matin de Paris
La pointe de la délivrance
L'espace du printemps naissant
La force idiote a le dessous
Ces esclaves nos ennemis
S'ils ont compris
S'ils sont capables de comprendre
Vont se lever.

1942

The weapons of sorrow [1944]

Once again it's morning a Paris morning
The moment of release
The space of nascent springtime
Idiot force is the loser
These slaves our enemies
If they have understood
If they are able to understand
Will get up and go away.

1942

AVIS

La nuit qui précéda sa mort
Fut la plus courte de sa vie
L'idée qu'il existait encore
Lui brûlait le sang aux poignets
Le poids de son corps l'écoeurait
Sa force le faisait gémir
C'est tout au fond de cette horreur
Qu'il a commencé à sourire
Il n'avait pas UN camarade
Mais des millions et des millions
Pour le venger il le savait
Et le jour se leva pour lui.

UN PETIT NOMBRE D'INTELLECTUELS FRANÇAIS S'EST MIS AU SERVICE DE L'ENNEMI

Epouvantés épouvantables
L'heure est venue de les compter
Car la fin de leur règne arrive
Ils nous ont vanté nos bourreaux
Ils nous ont détaillé le mal
Ils n'ont rien dit innocemment

Belles paroles d'alliance
Ils vous ont voilées de vermine
Leur bouche donne sur la mort

Mais voici que l'heure est venue
De s'aimer et de s'unir
Pour les vaincre et les punir.

NOTICE[1]

The night before his death
Was the shortest of his life
The idea that he was still alive
Made the blood burn in his wrists
The weight of his body made him sick
His strength made him moan
In the depths of that horror
He began to smile
He had not only ONE
But millions of comrades
To avenge him he knew it
And dawn rose for him.

A SMALL NUMBER OF FRENCH INTELLECTUALS PUT THEMSELVES AT THE SERVICE OF THE ENEMY

Horrified horrifying
The hour has come to count them
For the end of their reign is here
They praised our hangmen
They parcelled out the evil
They said nothing in innocence

Fine words of alliance
They have veiled in vermin
Their mouths look out on death

But now the time has come
To love each other and unite
To overcome and punish them.

---

[1] "On the walls of Paris, Notices, threats or lists of hostages, were pasted, producing fear in some and shame in all, Eluard wrote in *Raisons d'écrire.*

Au rendez-vous allemand [1944]

COMPRENNE QUI VOUDRA

En ce temps-là, pour ne pas châtier
les coupables, on maltraitait des filles
On allait même jusqu'à les tondre.

Comprenne qui voudra
Moi mon remords ce fut
La malheureuse qui resta
Sur le pavé
La victime raisonnable
A la robe déchirée
Au regard d'enfant perdue
Découronnée défigurée
Celle qui ressemble aux morts
Qui sont morts pour être aimés

Une fille faite pour un bouquet
Et couverte
Du noir crachat des ténébres

Une fille galante
Comme une aurore de premier mai
La plus aimable bête

Souillée et qui n'a pas compris
Qu'elle est souillée
Une bête prise au piége
Des amateurs de beauté
Et ma mére la femme
Voudrait bien dorloter
Cette image idéale
De son malheur sur terre.

At the German rendezvous [1944]

UNDERSTAND WHO WILL

> *In those days, so as not to punish*
> *the guilty, they maligned prostitutes.*
> *They even shaved their heads.*

Understand who will
My remorse was that
Unfortunate young woman
On the pavement
The reasonable victim
Her dress torn
With the look of a lost child
Uncrowned disfigured
Who resembles the dead
Who have died for being loved

A girl made for a bouquet
Besmeared
With the black spittle of the shadows

A proud girl
Like dawn on the first May
The most lovable creature

Dishonored and who hasn't understood
That she is dishonored
A creature caught in the trap
Of the amateurs of beauty
And my mother's heart of woman
Would like to cradle
That perfect image
Of her misfortune on earth.

A L'ÉCHELLE HUMAINE

*à la mémoire du colonel Fabien et à
Laurent Casanova qui m'a si bien parlé de lui.*

On a tué un homme
Un homme un ancien enfant
Dans un grand paysage
Une tache de sang
Comme un soleil couchant
Un homme couronné
De femme et d'enfants
Tout un idéal d'homme
Pour notre éternité

Il est tombé
Et son coeur s'est vidé
Ses yeux se sont vidés
Sa tete s'est vidée
Ses mains se sont ouvertes
Sans une plainte
Car il croyait au bonheur
Des autres
Car il avait répété
Je t'aime sur tous les tons
À sa mère à sa gardienne
À sa complice à son alliée
À la vie
Et il allait au combat
Contre les bourreaux des siens
Contre l'idée d'ennemi

At the German rendezvous [1944]

ON THE HUMAN SCALE

*To the memory of Colonel Fabien[1] and to
Laurent Casanova who spoke so well of him.*

They killed a man
A man once a child
In a vast countryside
A spot of blood
Like a setting sun
A man crowned by
A woman and children
A wholly ideal man
For our eternity

He is fallen
And his heart empties
His eyes emptied
His head emptied
His hands opened
Without a complaint
For he believed
In the happiness of others
For he had repeated
I love you in every tone
To his mother to his governess
To his helpmate to his ally
To life
He went to fight against
The butchers of his people
Against the idea of having enemies

---

[1] Colonel Fabien served in the International Brigades in Spain, returning to France after being severely wounded. He was Secretary of the Jeunesses Communistes de la Région Parisienne. By 1941, he had organized eighty percent of the actions of the French Resistance when he was shot, taken prisoner and cruelly tortured. A few months after his escape he was killed while directing the defense of a twelve-kilometer front in the Ardennes.

Et même les pires jours
Il avait chéri sa peine
Sa nature était d'aimer
Et de respecter la vie
Sa nature était la mienne

Rien qu'un seul jet de courage
Rien que la grandeur du peuple
Et je t'aime finit mal
Mais il affirme la vie
Je t'aime c'était l'Espagne
Qui luttait pour le soleil
C'est la région parisienne
Avec ses chemins puérils
Avec ses enfants gentils

Et le premier attentat
Contre les soldats du mal
Contre la mort répugnante
C'est la premiére lumiére
Dans la nuit des malheureux
Lumière toujours parfaite
Lumière de relation
Ronde de plus en plus souple
Etendue et animée
Graine et fleur et fruit et graine
Et je t'aime finit bien
Pour les hommes de demain.

At the German rendezvous [1944]

Even on the worst days
He had nurtured his sorrow
His nature was to love
And to respect life
His nature was like mine

With but one surge of courage
With the bravery of the people
And I love you comes to a bad end
Yet he affirms life
I love you that was Spain
Fighting for the sun
It is the region of Paris
With her childlike pathways
With her gentle children

And the first attack
Against the soldiers of evil
Against repugnant death
Is the first light
In the night of the unfortunate
Perfect light
A light of relating
Round increasingly supple
Spread out and alive
Seed and flower and fruit and seed
And I love you ends well
For tomorrow's people.

FAIRE VIVRE

Ils étaient quelques-uns qui vivaient dans la nuit
En rêvant du ciel caressant
Ils étaient quelques-uns qui aimaient la forêt
Et qui croyaient au bois brûlant
L'odeur des fleurs les ravissait même de loin
La nudité de leurs désirs les recouvraient

Ils joignaient dans leur coeur le souffle mesuré
À ce rien d'ambition de la vie naturelle
Qui grandit dans l'été comme un été plus fort

Ils joignaient dans leur coeur l'espoir du temps qui vient
Et qui salue même de loin un autre temps
À des amours plus obstinées que le désert

Un tout petit peu de sommeil
Les rendait au soleil futur
Ils duraient ils savaient que vivre perpétue

Et leurs besoins obscurs engendraient la clarté.

*

Ils n'étaient que quelques-uns
Ils furent foule soudain

Ceci est de tous les temps.

LET LIFE GO ON

There were a few who lived in the night
Dreaming of a caressing sky
There were a few who loved the forest
And believed in the burning wood
The scent of flowers delighted them from afar
The nakedness of their desires covered them

In their hearts they joined measured breathing
To that simple ambition for natural life
Which in summer grows like an even stronger summer

In their hearts they joined hope for a time to come
Hope that greets another time from a distance
With loves more obstinate than the desert

Just a little sleep
Restored them up to a future sun
They endured knowing that living perpetuates

And their obscure needs would engender light.

*

They were only a few
Suddenly they were a crowd

This is for all time.

Marc Chagall. The lovers. Lithograph. Illustration for
Le Dur désir de durer, 1950 edition. Coll. Musée Saint Denis.

IV

1946-1953

LE TEMPS DE LA RESOLUTION

THE TIME OF RESOLUTION

> *La résistance s'organise sur tous les fronts purs.*
> Tristan Tzara, *L'Antitête*, 1933.

> *Je dédie ces pages à ceux qui les liront mal*
> *et à ceux qui ne les aimeront pas.*
> Paul Eluard

. . .   .

Nue effacée ensommeillée
Choisie sublime solitaire
Profonde oblique matinale
Fraîche nacrée ébouriffée
Ravivée première régnante
Coquette vive passionnée
Orangée rose bleuissante
Jolie mignonne délurée
Naturelle couchée debout
Etreinte ouverte rassemblée
Rayonnante désaccordée
Gueuse rieuse ensorceleuse
Etincelante ressemblante
Sourde secrète souterraine
Aveugle rude désastreuse
Boisée herbeuse ensanglantée
Sauvage obscure balbutiante
Ensoleillée illuminée
Fleurie confuse caressante
Instruite discrète ingénieuse
Fidèle facile étoilée
Charnue opaque palpitante
Inaltérable contractée
Pavée construite vitrifiée
Globale haute populaire

> *Resistance is organizing on all pure brows.*
>
> Tristan Tzara, *L'Antitête*, 1933.

> *I dedicate these pages to those who will misinterpret them*
> *and to those who will not like them.*
>
> Paul Eluard

. . .   .

Naked wiped out drowsy [1]
Chosen sublime solitary
Profound oblique of the morning
Fresh pearled dishevelled
Refreshed primal reigning
Coquette lively impassioned
Orange tinted rose turning to blue
Pretty darling knowing
Natural lying standing
Hugged open gathered in
Dazzling discordant
Laughing enchanting wench
Sparkling resembling
Deaf secretive subterranean
Blind rough disastrous
Wooded grassy bloody
Wild obscure stammering
Sunny luminous
Blooming confused caressing
Informed discreet ingenious
Faithful easy starred
Fleshy opaque palpitating
Inalterable uptight
Paved constructed vitrified
Global lofty popular

---

[1] These adjectives, feminine in French, describe a woman; her voice later
interrupts the poet's.

Poésie ininterrompue [1946]

Barrée gardée contradictoire
Egale lourde métallique
Impitoyable impardonnable
Surprise dénouée rompue
Noire humiliée éclaboussée

Sommes-nous deux ou suis-je solitaire

Comme une femme solitaire
Qui dessine pour parler
Dans le désert
Et pour voir devant elle

L'année pourrait être heureuse
Un été en barres
Et l'hiver la neige est un lit bien fait
Quant au printemps on s'en détache
Avec des ailes bien formées

Revenue de la mort revenue de la vie
Je passe de juin à décembre
Par un miroir indifférent
Tout au creux de la vue

Comme une femme solitaire
Resterai-je ici-bas
Aurai-je un jour réponse à tout
Et réponse à personne

Le poids des murs ferme toutes les portes
Le poids des arbres épaissit la forêt
Va sur la pluie vers le ciel vertical
Rouge et semblable au sang qui noircira

Le soleil naît sur la tranche d'un fruit
La lune naît au sommet de mes seins
Le soleil fuit sur la rosée
La lune se limite

Barred guarded contradictory
Equal heavy metallic
Merciless unpardonable
Surprised unraveled broken
Black humiliated bespattered

Are we two or am I alone

Like a woman alone
Tracing pictures in the desert
To say what she means
And to see before her

The year might be happy
A summer in stripes
And winter snow is a well-made bed
From spring we free ourselves
With well-formed wings

Come back from death and from life
I pass from June to December
Through an indifferent mirror
In the hollow space of sight

Like a solitary woman
Shall I stay down here
Will I have an answer for everything one day
And a response to no one

The weight of walls shuts all the gates
The weight of trees thickens the forest
Rides on the rain toward the vertical sky
Red like blood that will blacken

The sun is born on a slice of fruit
The moon is born at the peak of my breasts
The sun escapes on the dew
The moon holds back

La vérité c'est que j'aimais
Et la vérité c'est que j'aime
De jour en jour l'amour me prend première
Pas de regrets j'ignore tout d'hier
Je ne ferai pas de progrès

Sur une autre bouche
Le temps me prendrait première

Et l'amour n'a pas le temps
Qui dessine dans le sable
Sous la langue des grands vents

Je parle en l'air
A demi-mot
Je me comprends
L'aube et la bouche où rit l'azur des nuits
Pour un petit sourire tendre
Mon enfant frais de ce matin
Que personne ne regarde

Mon miroir est détaché
De la grappe des miroirs
Une maille détachée
L'amour juste le reprend

Rien ne peut déranger l'ordre de la lumière
Où je ne suis que moi-même
Et ce que j'aime
Et sur la table
Ce pot plein d'eau et le pain du repos
Au fil des mains drapées d'eau claire
Au fil du pain fait pour la main friande
De l'eau fraîche et du pain chaud
Sur les deux versants du jour

The truth is that I loved
And the truth is that I love
From day to day love takes me first
No regrets I know nothing of yesterday
I shall make no progress

On another mouth
Time would take me first

And love hasn't time
That draws in the sand
Under the tongue of great winds

I'm talking to the wind
In half words
I understand myself
Dawn and mouth where azure night is laughing
For a tender little smile
My fresh morning child
That no one looks upon

My mirror is detached
From the cluster of mirrors
A stitch undone
Just love mends it

Nothing can disturb the order of light
Where I am none other but myself
And what I love
And on the table
This bowl of water and bread of repose
In the motion of these hands draped in clear water
In the current of bread made for sweet-loving hands
Cool water and warm bread
On both slopes on the day

Aujourd'hui lumière unique
Aujourd'hui l'enfance entière
Changeant la vie en lumière
Sans passé sans lendemain
Aujourd'hui rêve de nuit
Au grand jour tout se délivre
Aujourd'hui je suis toujours

Je serai la première et la seule sans cesse
Il n'y a pas de drame il n'y a que mes yeux
Qu'un songe tient ouverts
Ma chair est ma vertu
Elle multiplie mon image

Je suis ma mère et mon enfant
En chaque point de l'éternel
Mon teint devient plus clair mon tient devient plus sombre
Je suis mon rayon de soleil
Et je suis mon bonheur nocturne

Tous les mots sont d'accord
La boue est caressante
Quand la terre dégèle
Le ciel est souterrain
Quand il montre la mort
Le soir est matinal
Après un jour de peine

Mais l'homme
L'homme aux lentes barbaries
L'homme comme un marais
L'homme à l'instinct brouillé
A la chair en exil
L'homme aux clartés de serre
Aux yeux fermés l'homme aux éclairs
L'homme mortel et divisé
Au front siagnant d'espoir
L'homme en butte au passé

Today an unusual light
Today the whole of childhood
Changing life to light
Without a past or a tomorrow
Today a night's dream
In full daylight all is delivered
Today I am forever

I shall be the first and only one unceasing
There's no tragedy there are just my eyes
That a dream keeps open
My flesh is my virtue
It multiplies my image

I am my mother and my child
At each point of the eternal
My skin lightens then darkens
I am my sun's ray
I am my nocturnal joy

All words agree
The mud is soothing
When the earth thaws
The sky is underground
When it reveals death
Evening is like morning
After a day of grief

But man
Man of slow violence
Man like a swamp
Man of confused instinct
His flesh is in exile
Man of greenhouse light
His eyes closed man of lightning
Man mortal and divided
His brow bleeding with hope
Man blocked by the past

Et qui toujours regrette
Isolé quotidien
Dénué responsable

Savoir vieillir savoir passer le temps

Savoir régner savoir durer savoir revivre
Il rejeta ses draps il éclaira la chambre
Il ouvrit les miroirs légers de sa jeunesse
Et les longues allées qui l'avaient reconduit

Être un enfant être une plume à sa naissance
Être la source invariable et transparente
Toujours être au coeur blanc une goutte de sang
Une goutte de feu toujours renouvelée

Mordre un rire innocent mordre à même la vie
Rien n'a changé candeur rien n'a changé désir
L'hiver j'ai mon soleil il fait fleurir ma neige
Et l'été qui sent bon a toutes les faiblesses

L'on m'aimera car j'aime par-dessus tout ordre
Et je suis prêt à tout pour l'avenir de tous
Et je ne connais rien à l'avenir
Mais j'aime pour aimer et je mourrai d'amour

Il se mit à genoux pour un premier baiser
La nuit était pareille à la nuit d'autrefois
Et ce fut le départ et la fin du passé
La conscience amère qu'il avait vécu

Alors il réveilla les ombres endormies
La cendre grise et froide d'un murmure tu
La cendre de l'aveugle et la stérilité
Le jour sans espérance et la nuit sans sommeil

L'égale pauvreté d'une vie limitée

Who mourns for what has been
Isolated everyday man
Divested responsible

To know how to grow old how to pass the time

To know how to rule how to endure how to live again
He tossed back the sheets let light into his room
He opened the light mirrors of his youth
And the long pathways that had brought him back

To be a child a feather at its birth
To be the invariable transparent source
Always a drop of blood in a white heart
A drop of fire ever renewed

To bite innocent laughter even life itself
Nothing has changed candor nothing has changed desire
In winter I have my sun it makes my snow blossom
And summer that smells good to all weaknesses

I shall be loved for I love beyond all order
I am ready for anything for the future of all
I know nothing of the future
But I love for the sake of loving and shall die of love

He knelt down for a first kiss
The night was like the night of long ago
This was the departure the end of the past
The bitter conscience he had lived

Then he awakened the sleeping shadows
The cold grey ashes of a murmur silenced
Ashes of the blind and the sterility
Of hopeless day and sleepless night

Equal poverty of a limited life

Tous les mots se reflètent
Et les larmes aussi
Dans la force perdue
Dans la force rêvée

Hier c'est la jeunesse hier c'est la promesse

Pour qu'un seul baiser la retienne
Pour que l'entoure le plaisir
Comme un été blanc bleu et blanc
Pour qu'il lui soit règle d'or pur
Pour que sa gorge bouge douce
Sous la chaleur tirant la chair
Vers une caresse infinie

Pour qu'elle soit comme une plaine
Nue et visible de partout
Pour qu'elle soit comme une pluie
Miraculeuse sans nuage
Comme une pluie entre deux feux
Comme une larme entre deux rires

Pour qu'elle soit neige bénie
Sous l'aile tiède d'un oiseau
Lorsque le sang coule plus vite
Dans les veines du vent nouveau
Pour que ses paupières ouvertes
Approfondissent la lumière
Parfum total à son image
Pour que sa bouche et le silence
Intelligibles se comprennent
Pour que ses mains posent leur paume
Sur chaque tête qui s'éveille
Pour que les lignes de ses mains
Se continuent dans d'autres mains
Distances à passer le temps

Je fortifierai mon délire

All words reflect each other
And tears as well
In the lost strength
In the dreamed strength

Yesterday was youth yesterday the promise

So that one kiss may hold her
So that pleasure may surround her
Like a white blue and white summer
So it may be the measure of pure gold for her
So that her breast may softly move
Beneath the warmth drawing flesh
Towards an unending caresse

So that she may be like a prairie
Bare and visible from all around
Like a rainfall
Miraculous cloudless
Like rain between two fires
Like a tear between bursts of laughter
So she may be the blessed snow
Beneath a bird's warm wing
When blood flows faster
In the veins of the new wind
May her open eyelids
Deepen the light
All the perfume in her image
So that her hands may rest their palms
On each waking head
So that the lines in her hands
May continue in other hands
Distances beyone time

I shall fortify my delirium

De l'océan à la source
De la montagne à la plaine
Court le fantôme de la vie
L'ombre sordide de la mort
Mais entre nous
Une aube naît de chair ardente
Et bien précise
Qui remet la terre en état
Nous avançons d'un pas tranquille
Et la nature nous salue
Le jour incarne nos couleurs
Le feu nos yeux et la mer notre union
Et tous les vivants nous ressemblent
Tous les vivants que nous aimons

Les autres sont imaginaires
Faux et cernés de leur néant
Mais il nous faut lutter contre eux
Ils vivent à coups de poignards
Ils parlent comme un meuble craque
Leurs lèvres tremblent de plaisir
A l'écho des cloches de plomb
A la mutité d'un or noir

Un coeur seul pas de coeur
Un seul coeur tous les coeurs
Et les corps chaque étoile
Dans un ciel plein d'étoiles
Dans la carrière en mouvement
De la lumière et des regards
Notre poids brillant sur terre
Patine de la volupté

A chanter des plages humaines
Pour toi la vivante que j'aime
Et pour tous ceux que nous aimons
Qui n'ont envie que de s'aimer

From the ocean to the spring
From the mountain to the plain
Runs the phantom of life
The sordid shadow of death
But between us
A dawn is born of ardent flesh
Quite specific
That puts the earth back in order
We go forward with a steady step
Nature greets us
The day wears our colors
The fire our eyes and the sea our union
And all the living resemble us
All the living we love

Others are imaginary
False encircled by their emptiness
But we must struggle against them
They live by the dagger's thrust
They speak like a creaking chair
Their lips tremble with pleasure
At the echo of leaden bells
At the silence of black gold

A heart alone no heart
One heart all hearts
And the bodies each star
In a sky full of stars
In the moving course
Of light and of glances
Our weight shining on earth
Voluptuous patina

To sing of human beaches
For you the living woman I love
And for all those we love
Who only want to love each other

Je finirai bien par barrer la route
Au flot des rêves imposés
Je finirai bien par me retrouver
Nous prendrons possession du monde

O rire végétal ouvrant une clairière
De gorges chantonnant interminablement
Mains où le sang s'est effacé
Où l'innocence est volontaire
Gaieté gagnée tendresse du bois mort
Chaleurs d'hiver pulpes séchées
Fraicheurs d'été sortant des fleurs nouvelles
Constant amour multiplié tout nu

Rien à haïr et rien à pardonner
Aucun destin n'illustre notre front
Dans l'orage notre faiblesse
Est l'aiguille la plus sensible
Et la raison de l'orage
Image ô contact parfait
L'espace est notre milieu
Et le temps notre horizon

Quelques cailloux sur un sentier battu
De l'herbe comme un souvenir vague
Le ciel couvert et la nuit en avance
Quelques vitrines étrennant leurs lampes
Des trous la porte et la fenêtre ouvertes
Sur des gens qui sont emfermés
Un petit bar vendu et revendu
Apothéose de chiffres
Et de soucis et de mains sales

Un désastre profond
Où tout est mesuré même la tristesse
Même la dérision
Même la honte

I shall finally block the road
Against the flood of inflicted dreams
I shall find myself again
We shall take charge of the world

O vegetal laughter opening a clearing
Of throats singing endlessly
Hands wiped clean of blood
Where innocence is voluntary
Gaity earned like the tenderness of dead wood
Winter heat dried pulp
Summer cool coming from new flowers
Constant love multiplied stripped bare

Nothing to hate nothing to forgive
No destiny shines on our foreheads
In the storm our frailty
Is the most sensitive needle
And the reason for the storm
The image our perfect contact
Space is our milieu
And time our horizon

A few pebbles on a beaten path
Of grass like a vague memory
Sky overcast night coming on
A few shop windows try on their lamps
Holes the door and window opened
Onto people within
A little bar sold and sold again
Apotheosis of ciphers
Of worries and of dirty hands

A profound disaster
Where all is measured even sadness
Even derision
Even shame

La plainte est inutile
Le rire est imbécile
Le désert des taches grandit
Mieux que sur un suaire

Les yeux ont disparu les oiseaux volent bas
On n'entend plus le bruit des pas
Le silence est comme une boue
Pour les projets sans lendemain
Et soudain un enfant crie
Dans la cage de son ennui
Un enfant remue des cendres
Et rien de vivant ne bouge

Je rends compte du réel
Je prends garde à mes paroles
Je ne veux pas me tromper
Je veux savoir d'où je pars
Pour conserver tant d'espoir

Mes origines sont les larmes
Et la fatigue et la douleur
Et le moins de beauté
Et le moins de bonté

Le regret d'être au monde et l'amour sans vertu
M'ont enfanté dans la misère
Comme un murmure comme une ombre
Ils mourront ils sont morts
Mais ils vivront glorieux
Sable dans le cristal
Nourricier malgré lui
Plus clair qu'en plein soleil

Le regret d'être au monde

Je n'ai pas de regrets
Plus noir plus lourd est mon passé

Complaint is useless
Laughter is idiotic
The desert of stains grows
Better than on a shroud

Eyes have disappeared birds fly low
We no longer hear footsteps
The silence is like a mire
For plans with no future
Suddenly a child cries out
In the cage of his tedium
A child stirs the ashes
And nothing living moves

I take account of what's real
I am careful of my words
I will make no mistake
I want to know where I come from
To conserve so much hope

My origins are tears
Fatigue and sorrow
The least beauty
The least kindness

My regret for being in the world
Without selfless love I was born to poverty
Like a murmur like a shadow
They will die they are dead
But they will live in glory
Sand in the crystal
Nourishing inspite of itself
Brighter than in the full sun

Sorry to be born

I have no regrets
The blacker my past the heavier to bear

Plus léger et limpide est l'enfant que j'étais
L'enfant que je serai
Et la femme que je protège
La femme dont j'assume
L'éternelle confiance

Comme une femme solitaire
Qui dessine pour parler
Dans le désert
Et pour voir devant elle
Par charmes et caprices
Par promesses et abandons

Entr'ouverte à la vie
Toujours soulignée de bleu

Comme une femme solitaire
A force d'être l'une ou l'autre
Et tous les éléments

Je saurai dessiner comme mes mains épousent
La forme de mon corps
Je saurai dessiner comme le jour pénètre
Au fin fond de mes yeux

Et ma chaleur fera s'étendre les couleurs
Sur le lit de mes nuits
Sur la nature nue où je tiens une place
Plus grande que mes songes
Où je suis seule et nue où je suis l'absolu
L'être définitif
La première femme apparue
Le premier homme rencontré
Sortant du jeu qui les mêlait
Comme doigts d'une même main

The lighter and more limpid the child I was
The child I shall become
And the woman I protect
The woman whose eternal confidence
I assume

Like a solitary woman
Tracing pictures for words
In the wilderness
And to see before her
By charm and whim
By promises and abandon

Half open to life
Always underlined in blue

Like a solitary woman
By dint of being one or the other
And all the elements

I shall know how to draw as my hands take on
The form of my body
I shall know how to draw as daylight plumbs
The inner depths of my eyes

And my warmth will make the colors spread
On the bed of my nights
On bare nature where I take a more important place
Than my dreams
Where I am alone and naked I am the absolute
The definitive being
The first woman to appear
The first man encountered
Coming from the game which joined them
Like fingers of the same hand

La première femme étrangère
Et le premier homme inconnu
La première douleur exquise
Et le premier plaisir panique

Et la première différence
Entre des êtres fraternels
Et la première ressemblance
Entre des êtres différents

Le premier champ de neige vierge
Pour un enfant né en été
Le premier lait entre les lèvres
D'un fils de chair de sang secret

Buisson de roses et d'épines
Route de terre et de cailloux
À ciel ardent ciel consumé
À froid intense tête claire

Rocher de fardeaux et d'épaules
Lac de reflets et de poissons
À jour mauvais bonté remise
À mer immense voile lourde

Et j'écris pour marquer les années et les jours
Les heures et les hommes leur durée
Et les parties d'un corps commun
Qui a son matin
Et son midi et son minuit
Et de nouveau son matin
Inévitable et paré
De force et de faiblesse
De beauté de laideur
De repos agréable et de misérable lumière
Et de gloire provoquée

The first unfamiliar woman
And the first unknown man
The first exquisite pain
And the first fearful pleasure

And the first difference
Between fraternal beings
And the first resemblance
Between different beings

The first field of virgin snow
For a child born in summer
The first milk between the lips
Of a child of flesh of secret blood

Bush of roses and thorns
Road of dirt and pebbles
Under an ardent sky consumed
In intense cold clear headed

The crag of burdens to bear and shoulders
Lake of reflections and fish
Kindness restored on a bad day
Heavy sail on a vast sea

I write to mark the years and days
The hours and men their duration
And the parts of a common body
That has its morning
And its noon and its midnight
And again its morning
Inevitable and adorned
With strength and weakness
With beauty and homeliness
With pleasant rest and wretched light
With glory provoked

D'un matin sorti d'un rêve le pouvoir
De mener à bien la vie
Les matins passés les matins futurs
Et d'organiser le désastre
Et de séparer la cendre du feu

D'une maison les lumières naturelles
Et les ponts jetés sur l'aube
D'un matin la chair nouvelle
La chair intacte pétrie d'espoir
Dans la maison comme un glaçon qui fond

Du bonheur la vue sans pitié
Les yeux bien plantés sur leurs jambes
Dans la fumée de la santé
Du bonheur comme une règle
Comme un couteau impitoyable
Tranchant de tout
Sauf de la nécessité

D'une famille le coeur clos
Gravé d'un nom insignifiant

D'un rire la vertu comme un jeu sans perdants
Montagne et plaine
Calculées en tout point
Un cadeau contre un cadeau
Béatitudes s'annulant

D'un brasier les cloches d'or aux paupières lentes
Sur un paysage sans fin
Volière peinte dans l'azur
Et d'un sein supposé le poids sans réserves
Et d'un ventre accueillant la pensée sans raison
Et d'un brasier les cloches d'or aux yeux profonds
Dans un visage grave et pur

From morning out of a dream the power
To bring life to its fulfillment
Mornings past and future mornings
And to organize disaster
And to separate the ashes from the fire

From a house the natural lights
And the bridges thrown across dawn
From morning new flesh
Flesh intact kneaded by hope
In the house like a melting icicle

From happiness sight without pity
Eyes well planted on their legs
In the smoke of health
From happiness like a measure
Like a merciless knife
Cutting everything
Except necessity

From the closed heart of a family
Engraved with an insignificant name

Virtue from laughter a game without losers
Mountain and plain
Calculated on every point
A gift for a gift
Beatitudes annul each other

From the hearth coals golden bells with slow eyelids
Over an endless landscape
A birdhouse painted in the blue
And from a divined breast unreserved weight
And thought without reason from a welcoming womb
And from a hearthfire golden bells with deep eyes
In a face grave and pure

D'une volière peinte en bleu
Où les oiseaux sont des épis
Jetant leur or aux pauvres
Pour plus vite entrer dans le noir
Dans le silence hivernal

D'une rue
D'une rue ma défiguration
Au profit de tous et de toutes
Les inconnus dans la poussière
Ma solitude mon absence

D'une rue sans suite
Et sans saluts
Vitale
Et pourtant épuisante
La rencontre niée

De la fatigue le brouillard
Prolonge loques et misères
A l'intérieur de la poitrine
Et le vide aux tempes éteintes
Et le crépuscule aux artères

Du bonheur la vue chimérique
Comme au bord d'un abîme
Quand une grosse bulle blanche
Vous crève dans la tête
Et que le coeur est inutilement libre

Mais du bonheur promis et qui commence à deux
La première parole
Est déjà un refrain confiant
Contre la peur contre la faim
Un signe de ralliement

D'une main composée pour moi
Et qu'elle soit faible qu'importe

From a birdhouse painted blue
Where birds are spikes of wheat
Casting their gold to the poor
The quicker to enter darkness
In winter silence

Of a street
My disfiguration of a street
To everyone's profit
The unknown in the dust
My solitude my absence

Of a street without issue
And without greetings
Vital
Yet exhausting
The denied encounter

The fog of fatigue
Prolongs tears and miseries
Inside the chest
And the emptiness at the extinguished temples
And twilight in the arteries

The phantom sign of happiness
As on the edge of an abyss
When a great white bubble
Bursts in your head
When the heart is free to no avail

But of promised happiness beginning with two
The first word
Is already a trusting refrain
Against fear and hunger
A rallying sign

Of a hand composed for me
If it be weak what matter

Cette main double la mienne
Pour tout lier tout délivrer
Pour m'endormir pour m'éveiller

D'un baiser la nuit des grands rapports humains
Un corps auprès d'un autre corps
La nuit des grands rapports terrestres
La nuit native de ta bouche
La nuit où rien ne se sépare

Que ma parole pèse sur la nuit qui passe
Et que s'ouvre toujours la porte par laquelle
Tu es entrée dans ce poème
Porte de ton sourire et porte de ton corps

Par toi je vais de la lumière à la lumière
De la chaleur à la chaleur
C'est par toi que je parle et tu restes au centre
De tout comme un soleil consentant au bonheur

Mais il nous faut encore un peu
Accorder nos yeux clairs A ces nuits inhumaines
Des hommes qui n'ont pas trouvé la vie sur terre
Il nous faut qualifier leur sort pour les sauver

Nous partirons d'en bas nous partirons d'en haut
De la tête trop grosse et de la tête infime
En haut un rien de tête en bas l'enflure ignoble
En haut rien que du front en bas rien que menton
Rien que prison collant aux os
Rien que chair vague et que poisons gobés
Par la beauté par la laideur sans répugnance
Toujours un oeil aveugle une langue muete
Une main inutile un coeur sans résonance
Près d'une langue experte et qui voit loin
Près d'un oeil éloquent près d'une main prodigue
Trop près d'un coeur qui fait la loi

This hand doubles my own
To tie all together to deliver all
To let me sleep to awaken me

The night of great human affinities from a kiss
One body near another body
The night of great earthly affinities
The native night of your mouth
Night where nothing comes apart

May my word weigh on the passing night
And may the door be ever open
By which you entered in this poem
Door of your smile door of your body

Through you I go from light to light
From warmth to warmth
I speak through you and you stay at the center
Of it all like a sun consenting to happiness

But we need still more
To reconcile our clear eyes to the inhuman nights
Of men who have not found life on earth
We must qualify their fate to save them

We shall start from below or from above
From the swollen head and the small mind
Above mindless below the ignoble swelling
Only a brow above only a chin below
Nothing but prison clinging to the bones
Nothing but vague flesh and poison swallowed
By beauty and ugliness without repugnance
Always a blind eye a muted tongue
A useless hand a heart without resonance
Near an expert far-seeing tongue
Near an eloquent eye near a prodigal hand
Too near a heart which makes the law

La loi la feuille morte et la voile tombée
La loi la lampe éteinte et le plaisir gâché
La nourriture sacrifiée l'amour absurd
La neige sale et l'aile inerte et la vieillesse

Sur les champs un ciel étroit
Soc du néant sur les tombes

Au tournant les chiens hurlant
Vers une carcasse folle

Au tournant l'eau est crépue
Et les champs claquent des dents

Et les chiens sont des torchons
Léchant des vitres brisées

Sur les champs la puanteur
Roule noire et bien musclée

Sur le ciel tout ébréché
Les étoiles sont moisies

Allez donc penser à l'homme
Allez donc faire un enfant

Allez donc pleurer ou rire
Dans ce monde de buvard

Prendre forme dans l'informe
Prendre empreinte dans le flou

Prendre sens dans l'insensé
Dans ce monde sans espoir

Si nous montions d'un degré

Le jour coule come un oeuf
Le vent fané s'effiloche

Toute victoire est semblable
Des ennemis des amis

The law dead leaf and fallen veil
The law burnt-out lamp and spoiled pleasure
Food sacrificed and absurd love
Dirty snow and the inert wing and old age

Above the fields a narrow sky
Plowshare of the void above the tombs

At the turning howling dogs
At a maddened carcass

At the turning the water is wrinkled
And the fields' teeth are chattering

And the dogs are rags
Licking broken windows

The stench rolls black muscular
Over the fields

In a jagged sky
The stars are moldy

Go on think about man
Go on make a child

Go on laugh or cry
In this world like a blotter

Take on form in the formless
Make an impression in the flux

To make sense out of the senseless
In this world without hope

Suppose we rise by one degree

Day flows like an egg
The faded wind unravels

Every victory is the same
For enemies or for friends

Ennemis amis pâlots
Que même le repos blesse

Et de leurs drapeaux passés
Ils enveloppent leurs crampes

Beaux oiseaux évaporés
Ils rêvent de leurs pensées

Ils se tissent des chapeaux
Cent fois plus grands que leur tête

Ils méditent leur absence
Et se cachent dans leur ombre

Ils ont été au présent
Ceci entre parenthèse

Ils croient qu'ils ont été des diables des lionceaux
Des chasseurs vigoureux des nègres transparents
Des intrus sans vergogne et des rustres impurs
Des monstres opalins et des zèbres pas mal

Des anonymes redoutables
Des calembours et des charades

Et la ligne de flottaison
Sur le fleuve héraclitéen

Et l'hospitalité amère
Dans un asile carnassier

Et le désonneur familial
Et le point sec des abreuvoirs

Ils croient ils croient mais entre nous
Il vaut encore mieux qu'ils croient

Si nous montions d'un gré

Uninterrupted poetry   [1946]

Enemies pallid friends
Wounded even by rest

And with their faded banners
They wrap their cramps

Beautiful evaporated birds
They dream their thoughts

They weave their hats
A hundred times bigger than their heads

They mediate their absence
And hide in their shadows

They have been in the present
That's just by the way

They believe they've been devils' lion-cubs
Mighty hunters transparent negroes
Shameless intruders and impure clowns
Opaline monsters and pretty nice zebras

Formidable unknowns
Puns and charades

And the high water mark
On the Heraclitean river

And bitter hospitality
In a wild beast's den

And family dishonor
And the dry point of watering troughs

They believe they do believe but just between us
It's better that they believe

Suppose we rise by one degree

Poésie ininterrompue [1946]

C'est la santé l'élégance
En dessous roses et noirs

Rousseurs chaudes blancheurs sobres
Rien de gros rien de brumeux

Les coquilles dans la nuit
D'un piano sans fondations

Les voitures confortables
Aux roues comme des guirlandes

C'est le luxe des bagages
Blasés jetés à la mer

Et l'aisance du langage
Digéré comme un clou par un mur

Les idées à la rigolade
Des désirs à l'office

Une poule un vin la merde
Réchauffés entretenus

Si nous montions d'un degré
Dans ce monde sans images

Vers la plainte d'un berger
Qui est seul et qui a froid

Vers une main généreuse
Qui se tend et que l'on souille

Vers un aveugle humilié
De se cogner aux fenêtres

Vers l'excuse désolée
D'un maleureux sans excuses

216

It's health and elegance
Pink and black underneath
Warm rusty colors sober white
Nothing gross nothing foggy

The seashells at night
Of a piano without underpinnings

Comfortable carriages
With wheels like garlands

It's the luxury of baggage
Careless thrown out to sea

And the ease of language
Digested like a nail in a wall

Ideas giggling
Desires in church

A chicken a glass of wine a turd
Warmed over saved

Suppose we rise by one degree
In this world without pictures

Towards the moaning of a shepherd
Cold and alone

Towards a generous hand
Extended and spat upon

To a blind man humiliated
For stumbling against windows

To the sorrowful excuse
Of a wretch with no excuse

Vers le bavardage bête
Des victimes consolées

Semaines dimanches lâches
Qui s'épanchent dans le vide

Durs travaux loisirs gâchés
Peaux grises résorbant l'homme

Moralité de fourmi
Sous les pieds d'un plus petit

Si nous montions d'un degré

La misère s'éternise
La cruauté s'assouvit

Les guerres s'immobilisent
Sur les glaciers opulents

Entre les armes en broussailles
Sèchent la viande et le sang

De quoi calmer les âmes amoureuses
De quoi varier le cours des rêveries

De quoi provoquer l'oubli
Aussi de quoi changer la loi

La loi la raison pratique

Et que comprendre juge
L'erreur selon l'erreur

Si voir était la foudre
Au pays des charognes

Le juge serait dieu
Il n'y a pas de dieu

Si nous montions d'un degré

To the silly chatter
Of victims consoled

Weeks cowardly Sundays
Poured into the emptiness

Hard labor spoiled pleasure
Grey skins absorbing man

Morality of the ant
Under the feet of one smaller

If we should go up one degree

Misery becomes eternal
Cruelty is glutted

Wars are immobilized
On opulent glaciers

Meat and blood are drying
Between weapons in the undercover

It's enough to calm amorous souls
It's enough to change the course of reveries

Enough to bring on forgetfulness
As well as enough to change the law

The law of practical reason

And let understanding judge
Error according to the error

If seeing were lightning
In the land of corpses

The judge would be a god
There is no god

Suppose we go up one degree

Vers l'extase sans racines
Toute bleu j'en suis payé

Aussi bien que de cantiques
Et de marches militaires

Et de mots définitifs
Et de bravos entraînants

Et la secousse idéale
De la vanité sauvage

Et le bruit insupportable
Des objecteurs adaptés

Le golfe d'une serrure
Abrite trop de calculs

Et je tremble comme un arbre
Au passage des saisons

Ma sève n'est qu'une excuse
Mon sang n'est qu'une raison

Si nous montions d'un degré

Mes vieux amis mon vieux Paul
Il faut avouer

Tout avouer et non seulement le désespoir
Vice des faibles sans sommeil

Et pas seulement nos rêves
Vertu des forts anéantis

Mais le reflet brouillé la vilaine blessure
Du voyant dénaturé

Vous acceptez j'accepte d'être infirme
La même sueur baigne notre suicide

To a rootless ecstasy true blue
I have received my reward from it

As well as canticles
And military marches

And definitive words
And captivating bravos

And ideal shock
Of savage vanity

And the intolerable noise
Of conforming objectors

The gulf of a lock
Shelters too much calculation

And I tremble like a tree
At the seasons' passing

My sap is only an excuse
My blood is only one reason

Suppose we rise by one degree

My old friends my old Paul
We must confess

Everything not only our despair
Vice of the sleepless weak

And not only our dreams
Virtue of destroyed strong-men

But the clouded reflection and ugly wound
Of the denatured prophet

You accept I accept our infirmity
The same sweat bathes our suicide

Mes vieux amis

Vieux innocents et vieux coupables
Dressés contre la solitude

Où s'allume notre folie
Où s'accuse notre impatience

Nous ne sommes seuls qu'ensemble
Nos amours se contredisent

Nous exigeons tout de rien
L'exception devient banale

Mais notre douleur aussi
Et notre déchéance

Nous nous réveillons impurs
Nous nous révélons obscurs

Brutes mentales du chaos
Vapeurs unique de l'abîme

Dans la basse région lyrique
Où nous nous sommes réunis

Mes vieux amis pour être séparés
Pour être plus nombreux

Si nous montions d'un degré

Sur des filles couronnées
Une épave prend le large

A l'orient de mon destin
Aurai-je un frère demain

My old friends

Old innocents and guilty ones
Trained against solitude

Where our madness is lit
Where our impatience is marked

We are alone only when we are together
Our loves are contradictory

We demand everything from nothing
The exception becomes commonplace

So does our sorrow
And our decadence

We awaken impure
We reveal ourselves obscure

Mental brutes of chaos
Unique vapors from the abyss

In the low lyrical region
Where we gathered together

My old friends for being apart
For being more numerous

Suppose we go up one degree

On crowned girls
A derelict takes to the open sea

To the orient of my destiny
Will I have a brother tomorrow

Sur des ruines virginales
Aux ailes de papillon

Friandises de l'hiver
Quand la mère joue la morte

Sans passion et sans dégoût
Une ruche couve lourde
Dans une poche gluante

Paume attachée à son bien
Comme la cruche à son eau
Et le printemps aux bourgeons

Fer épousé par la forge
Or maté en chambre forte

Nue inverse rocher souple
D'où rebondit la cascade

Simulacre du sein
Livré aux égoistes

Mais aussi le sein offert
De l'image reconquise

Plaisir complet plaisir austère
Pommier noir aux pommes mûres

Belle belle rôde et jouit
Fluorescente dentelle

Où l'éclair est une aiguille
La pluie le fil

L'aile gauche du coeur
Se replie sur le coeur

On virginal ruins
With butterfly's wings

Sweetmeats of winter
When the mother plays dead

Without passion without disgust
A beehive broods heavy
In a sticky pocket

The palm attached to its goods
As the pitcher to its water
And springtime to its buds

Iron wedded by the forge
Gold dulled in a crucible

Inverse cloud supple cliff
Where the waterfall leaps back

The likeness of a breast
Delivered to egotists

But as well the proffered breast
Of the image rediscovered

Complete pleasure austere pleasure
Black apple tree with ripe apples

Beauty beauty roves and enjoys
Fluorescent lace

Where lightning is a needle
The rain is the thread

The left wing of the heart
Folds back on the heart

Je vois brûler l'eau pure et l'herbe du matin
Je vais de fleur en fleur sur un corps auroral
Midi qui dort je veux l'entourer de clameurs
L'honorer dans son jour de senteurs de lueurs

Je ne me méfie plus je suis le fils de femme
La vacance de l'homme et le temps bonifié
La réplique grandiloquente
Des étoiles minuscules

Et nous montons

Les derniers arguments du néant sont vaincus
Et le dernier bourdonnement
Des pas revenant sur eux-mêmes

Peu à peu se décomposent
Les alphabets ânonnés
De l'histoire et des morales
Et la syntaxe soumise
Des souvenirs enseignés

Et c'est très vite
La liberté conquise
La liberté feuille de mai
Chauffée à blanc
Et le feu aux nuages
Et le feu aux oiseaux
Et le feu dans les caves
Et les hommes dehors
Et les hommes partout
Tenant toute la place
Abattant les murailles
Se partageant le pain
Dévêtant le soleil
S'embrassant sur le front
Habillant les orages
Et s'embrassant les mains

I see pure water burning and morning grass
I go from flower to flower on a body of daybreak
Sleeping noon I will encircle with shouting
To honor it in its day of perfumes and soft light

I no longer doubt I am a woman's son
Man's holiday time made good
The grandiloquent reply
Of minuscule stars

And we go higher

The last arguments of nothingness are overcome
And the last buzzing
Of steps turning on themselves

Decomposed little by little
Are the stammering alphabets
Of history and of morals
And the submissive syntax
Of taught memories

And quickly
Liberty is won
May-leaf liberty
Heated white
And fire in the clouds
And fire with birds
Fire in the cellars
And men outside
And men everywhere
Filling the village square
Breaking down the walls

Sharing the bread
Unveiling the sun
Kissing the forehead
Dressing up the tempests
Kissing hands

Faisant fleurir charnel
Et le temps et l'espace

Faisant chanter les verrous
Et respirer les poitrines

Les prunelles s'écarquillent
Les cachettes se dévoilent
La pauvreté rit aux larmes
De ses chagrins ridicules
Et minuit mûrit des fruits
Et midi mûrit des lunes

Tout se vide et se remplit
Au rythme de l'infini
Et disons la vérité
La jeunesse est un trésor
La vieillesse est un trésor
L'océan est un trésor
Et la terre est une mine
L'hiver est une fourrure
L'été une boisson fraîche
Et l'automne un lait d'accueil

Quant au printemps c'est l'aube
Et la bouche c'est l'aube
Et les yeux immortels
Ont la forme de tout

Nous deux toi toute nue
Moi tel que j'ai vécu
Toi la source du sang
Et moi les mains ouvertes
Comme des yeux

Nous deux nous ne vivons que pour être fidèles
A la vie
. . .   .

Making the flesh bloom
As well as time and space

Making the lock bolts sing
And lungs breathe

Eyes open wide
The hiding places are revealed
Poverty laughs to tears
Over its laughable worries
And midnight ripen fruits
And midday ripens moons

Everything is emptied and refilled
In the rhythm of the infinite
And to tell the truth
Youth is a treasure
Old age is a treasure
The ocean is a treasure
And the earth is a mine
Winter is a fur coat
Summer a cool drink
Autumn a welcoming glass of milk

Spring is the dawn
And one's mouth is the dawn
And immortal eyes
Take on the form of everything

We two and you naked
Myself such as I have lived
You the fountainhead of blood
I with my hands open
Just like eyes

We two live only to be faithful
To life

. . .   . ·   . . .   .

LE TRAVAIL DU POÈTE

à Guillevic

I

Les belles manières d'être avec les autres
Sur l'herbe pelée en été
Sous les nuages blancs

Les belles manières d'être avec les femmes
Dans une maison grise et chaude
Sous un drap transparent

Les belles manières d'être avec soi-même
Devant la feuille blanche

Sous la menace d'impuissance
Entre deux temps et deux espaces

Entre l'ennui et la manie de vivre

II

Qu'êtes-vous venu prendre
Dans la chambre familière

Un livre qu'on n'ouvre jamais

Qu'êtes-vous venu dire
À la femme indiscrète

Ce qu'on ne peut pas répéter

Qu'êtes-vous venu voir
Dans ce lieu bien en vue

Ce que voient les aveugles

THE POET'S WORK

to Guillevic[1]

I

Good manners in company
On stripped summer lawns
Under white clouds

Good manners with women
In a warm grey house
Under a transparent sheet

Good manners with one's self
Before a blank page

Under the menace of impotence
Between two times and two places

Between boredom and the zest for living

II

What did you come to get
In the familiar room

A book that's never opened

What did you come to say
To the indiscreet woman

That cannot be repeated

What did you come to see
In this most visible place

What the blind see

---

[1]Poet of the Resistance. His *Requiem* was published in 1938.

III

La route est courte
On arrive bien vite
Aux pierres de couleur
Puis
A la pierre vide

On arrive bien vite
Aux mots égaux
Aux mots sans poids
Puis
Aux mots sans suite

Parler sans avoir rien à dire
On a dépassé l'aube
Et ce n'est pas le jour
Et ce n'est pas la nuit
Rien c'est l'écho d'un pas sans fin

IV

Une année un jour lointains
Une promenade le coeur battant
Le paysage prolongeait
Nos paroles et nos gestes
L'allée s'en allait de nous
Les arbres nous grandissaient
Et nous calmions les rochers

C'est bien là que nous fûmes
Réglant toute chaleur
Toute clarté utile
C'est là que nous chantâmes
Le monde était intime
C'est là que nous aimâmes

Une foule nous précéda

III

The road is short
We come quickly
To the colorful rocks
Then
To the empty rock

We come quickly
To words that mean the same
To words lacking weight
Then to words without sequel

Talking with nothing to say
We have passed dawn
Yet it's neither day
Nor night nothing
But the echo of an endless footstep

IV

A year and a day long gone
Taking a walk heart beating
The landscape extended
Our words and gestures
The path was leading away from us
The trees made us grow
And we calmed the rocks

Surely that's where we were
Regulating all warmth
All useful light
There's where we sang
The world was intimate
There's where we loved

A crowd was there before us

Une foule nous suivit
Nous parcourut en chantant
Comme toujours quand le temps
Ne compte plus ni les hommes
Et que le coeur se repent
Et que le coeur se libère

V

Il y a plus longtemps encore
J'ai été seul
Et j'en frémis encore

Ô solitude simple
Ô négatrice du hasard charmant
J'avoue t'avoir connue

J'avoue avoir été abandonné
Et j'avoue même
Avoir abandonné ceux que j'aimais

Au cours des années tout s'est ordonné
Comme un ensemble de lueurs
Sur un fleuve de lumière
Comme les voiles des vaisseaux
Dans le beau temps protecteur
Comme les flammes dans le feu
Pour établir la chaleur

Au cours des années je t'ai retrouvée
Ô présence indéfinie
Volume espace de l'amour

Multiplié

. . . .

A crowd followed us
Looked us over singing
As always when time
And people don't matter any more
And the heart repents
And the heart earns its freedom

V

For a longer time now
I have been alone
I still shudder at the thought

Oh simple solitude
That denies intriguing chance
I confess having known you

I confess I was abandoned
I even abandoned
Those I loved

Over the years everything fell into place
Like an ensemble of glimmering lights
On a river of light
Like ships' sails
In the fine beneficent weather
Like the fire's flames
That bring warmth

During the years I found you again
Oh indefinite presence
Volume space of love

Multiplied

. . . .

VI

Je suis le jumeau des êtres que j'aime
Leur double en nature la meilleure preuve
De leur vérité je sauve la face
De ceux que j'ai choisis pour me justifier

Ils sont très nombreux ils sont innombrables
Ils vont par les rues pour eux et pour moi
Ils portent mon nom je porte le leur
Nous sommes les fruits semblables d'un arbre

Plus grand que nature et que toutes les preuves

VII

Je sais parce que je le dis
Que mes désires ont raison
Je ne veux pas que nous passions
A la boue
Je veux que le soleil agisse
Sur nos douleurs qu'il nous anime
Vertigineusement
Je veux que nos mains et nos yeux
Reviennent de l'horreur ouvertes pures

Je sais parce que je le dis
Que ma colère a raison
Le ciel a été foulé la chair de l'homme
A été mise en pièces
Glacée soumise dispersée

Je veux qu'on lui rende justice
Une justice sans pitié
Que l'on frappe en plein visage les bourreaux
Les maîtres sans racines parmi nous

VI

I am the twin of those I love
Their double in nature the best proof
Of their truth I save the face
Of those I have chosen to justify myself

There are so many they cannot be named
They go their way for themselves and for me
They bear my name I take theirs
We are similar fruits of one tree

Bigger than nature bigger than all evidence

VII

I know because I say so
That my hopes are justified
I don't want us to turn
To mud
I want the sun to work
On our suffering to bring us back to life
Dizzily
I want our hands and eyes to return
Open and pure from the horror

I know because I say so
That my anger is justified
The sky has been trampled
Human flesh rent asunder
Frozen subjugated dispersed

I would have justice done
Justice without pity
Let them strike the butchers in the face
The rootless masters in our midst

Je sais parce que je le dis
Que mon désespoir a tort
Il y a partout des ventres tendres
Pour inventer des hommes
Pareils à moi
Mon orgueil n'a pas tort
Le monde ancien ne peut me toucher je suis libre
Je ne suis pas un fils de roi je suis un homme
Debout qu'on a voulu abattre

Uninterrupted poetry   [1946]

I know because I tell you
That my despair is wrong
There are tender bellies everywhere
For inventing men
Like me
My pride is not wrong
The former world cannot touch me I am free
I am not a king's son I am a man standing
Whom they wanted to strike down

LE TRAVAIL DU PEINTRE

À Pablo Picasso

I

Entoure ce citron de blanc d'oeuf informe
Enrobe ce blanc d'oeuf d'un azur souple et fin
La ligne droite et noire a beau venir de toi
L'aube est derrière ton tableau

Et des murs innombrable croulent
Derrière ton tableau et toi l'oeil fixe
Comme un aveugle comme un fou
Tu dresses une haute épée vers le vide

Une main pourquoi pas une seconde main
Et pourquoi pas la bouche nue comme une plume
Pourquoi pas un sourire et pourquoi pas des larmes
Tout au bord de la toile où jouent les petits clous

Voici le jour d'autrui laisse aux ombres leur chance
Et d'un seul mouvement des paupières renonce

II

Tu dressais une haute épée
Comme un drapeau au vent contraire
Tu dressais ton regard contre l'ombre et le vent
Des ténèbres confondantes

Tu n'as pas voulu partager
Il n'y a rien à attendre de rien
La pierre ne tombera pas sur toi
Ni l'éloge complaisant

Dur contempteur avance en renoncant
Le plaisir naît au sein de ton refus
L'art pourrait être une grimace
Tu le réduis à n'être qu'une porte

Ouverte par laquelle entre la vie

THE PAINTER'S WORK

To Pablo Picasso

I

Wrap this lemon with a formless white of egg
Coat this white of egg with a fine supple azure
The straight black line surely could not be yours
Dawn is behind your painting

And innumerable walls are crumbling
Behind your painting and you staring
Like a blind man like a madman
You raise a high sword toward the void

One hand why not another
And why not the bare mouth like a feather
Why not a smile why not tears at the very edge
Of the canvas where the little nails are playing

Here is a day for others leave the shadows to their luck
With a blink give them up

II

You raised a sword high
Like a flag against the wind
You raised your eyes to the shadow and wind
Disconcerting shadows

You did not want to compromise
There's nothing to expect of anything
The rock will not fall on you
Nor complacent praise

Hard contemptuous man go forth renouncing
In the heart of your refusal pleasure is born
Art could be a grimace
You reduce it to be only an open door

Through which life enters

III

Et l'image conventionnelle du raisin
Posé sur le tapis l'image
Conventionnelle de l'épée
Dressée vers le vide point d'exclamation
Point de stupeur et d'hébétude
Qui donc pourra me la reprocher

Qui donc pourra te reprocher la pose
Immémoriale de tout homme en proie à l'ombre
Les autres sont de l'ombre mais les autres portent
Un fardeau aussi lourd que le tien
Tu es une des branches de l'étoile d'ombre
Qui détermine la lumière

Ils ne nous font pas rire ceux qui parlent d'ombre
Dans les souterrains de la mort
Ceux qui croient au désastre et qui charment leur mort
De mille et une vanités sans une épine
Nous nous portons notre sac de charbon
A l'incendie qui nous confond

IV

Tout commence par des images
Disaient les fous frères de rien
Moi je relie par des images
Toutes les aubes au grand jour

J'ai la meilleure conscience
De nos désirs ils sont gentils
Doux et violents comme des faux
Dans l'herbe tendre et rougissante

Aujourd'hui nous voulons manger
Ensemble ou bien jouer et rire
Aujourd'hui je voudrais aller
En U.R.S.S. ou bien me reposer

III

And the conventional image of the grape
Placed on the rug the conventional image
Of the sword raised
Toward empty space exclamation point
Not stupor no bewilderment
Who then can reproach me for it

Who then can reproach you for the immemorial pose
Of everyone who is prey to the shadow
The others are of the shadow but they bear
A burden as heavy as yours
You are one branch of the shadowy star
Who determines light

Those who speak of shadows in death's underworld
Who believe in disaster and charm their death
With a thousand and one vanities without a thorn
Don't make us laugh
We carry our own bag of coal
To the fire that consumes us

IV

Everything begins with images
So said the mad brothers of nothing
I for one tie all the dawns together
With images in full light of day

I am fully aware
Of our well-intended desires
Gentle and violent like scythes
In the tender blushing grass

Today we want to break bread
Together or laugh and play
Today I'd like to go
To the U.S.S.R. or take it easy

Avec mon coeur à l'épousée
Avec le pouvoir de bien faire
Et l'espoir fort comme une gerbe
De mains liées sur un baiser

V

Picasso mon ami dément
Mon ami sage hors frontières
Il n'y a rien sur notre terre
Qui ne soit plus pur que ton nom

J'aime à le dire j'aime à dire
Que tous tes gestes sont signés
Car à partir de là les hommes
Sont justifiés à leur grandeur

Et leur grandeur est différente
Et leur grandeur est tout égale
Elle se tient sur le pavé
Elle se tient sur leurs désirs

VI

Toujours c'est une affaire d'algues
De chevelures de terrains
Une affaire d'amis sincères
Avec des fièvres de fruits mûrs

De morts anciennes de fleurs jeunes
Dans des bouquets incorruptibles
Et la vie donne tout son coeur
Et la mort donne son secret

Une affaire d'amis sincères
À travers les âges parents
La création quotidienne
Dans le bonjour indifférent

Uninterrupted poetry [1946]

With my heart given to my bride
With the power of doing good
And hope strong as a new sheaf
Of hands bound together on a kiss

V

Picasso my mad friend
My friend wise beyond frontiers
There is nothing on our earth
Purer than your name

I like to say so I like to say
That your every gesture is signed
By that men measure up
To their greatness

Their greatness is different
Their greatness is all the same
It is maintained on the streets
It is maintained in their desires

VI

It is always a matter of seaweed
Of heads of hair of territories
An agreement among true friends
With fevers of ripe fruit

Of deaths long past of flowers of youth
In incorruptible bouquets
And life gives its whole heart
And death gives its secret

An agreement of true friends
Across related ages
The daily creation
In the indifferent hello

VII

Rideau il n'y a pas de rideau
Mais quelques marches à monter
Quelques marches à construire
Sans fatigue et sans soucis
Le travail deviendra un plaisir
Nous n'en avons jamais douté nous savons bien
Que la souffrance est en surcharge et nous voulons
Des textes neufs des toiles vierges après l'amour

Des yeux comme des enclumes
La vue comme l'horizon
Des mains au seuil de connaître
Comme biscuits dans du vin

Et le seul but d'être premier partout
Jour partagé caresse sans degré
Cher camarade à toi d'être premier
Dernier au monde en un monde premier.

VII

A curtain there is no curtain
Only a few steps to climb
A few steps to build
Tireless and free of cares
Work will become a pleasure
We never doubted it we know very well
That suffering is a surfeit we want
New texts virgin canvases after love

Eyes like anvils
Vision like the horizon
Hands at the threshold of recognition
Like biscuits in wine

And the only goal being first everywhere
The day shared an unmeasured caress
Dear comrade it is for you to be first
And last in a new world.

À L'ÉCHELLE ANIMALE

Cette petite tache de lumière dans la campagne
Ce feu du soir est un serpent à la tête froide
La tache de la bête dans un paysage humain
Où tous les animaux sont les mouvements
De la terre bien réelle
Du soleil maigre et pâle
Du soleil gros et rouge
Et de la lune sans passé
Et de la lune à souvenirs

Cette petite tache de lumière cette fenêtre
Eclaire les épaules adorables d'un ours
Et d'un loup de Paris vieux de mille ans
Et d'un furieux sanglier d'aujourd'hui
Et d'un lièvre qui fuit comme un innocent

La forêt voilà la forêt
Malgré la nuit je la vois
Je la touche je la connais
Je fais la chasse à la forêt
Elle s'éclaire d'elle-même
Par ses frissons et par ses voix

Chaque arbre d'ombre et de reflets
Est un miroir pour les oiseaux
Et la rivière la rivière
Dont les poissons sont les bergers
Quelle rivière bien dressée

Voir clair dans l'oeil droit des hiboux
Voir clair dans les gouttes de houx
Dans le terrier fourré d'obscurité fondante
Voir clair dans la main des taupes
Dans l'aile étendue très haut
Dans le gui des philosophes
Dans le tout cela des savants

ON THE ANIMAL SCALE

This little spot of light in the countryside
This evening fire is a cold-headed serpent
The spot of the beast in a human landscape
Where all the animals are motions
Of the very real earth
Of the thin pale sun
Of the fat red sun
Of the moon without a past
And of the moon of memories

This little spot of light this window
Illumines the adorable shoulders of a bear
Of a Parisian wolf a thousand years old
Of the angry wild boar of today
Of a hare fleeing like an innocent

Over there is the forest
Inspite of night I see it
I touch it I know it
I go hunting for the forest
It lights up by itself
By its shivers and its voices

Every tree of shadow and reflections
Is a mirror for the birds
And the river the river
Whose fish are its keepers
What a well trained river

To see clearly in the owl's right eye
To see clearly in drops of holly
In the fur-lined burrow of melting obscurity
To see clearly in the hand of moles
In the wing stretched high
In the mistletoe of the philosophers
In the attributes of the sages

Monde connu et naturel

Voir clair et se reconnaître
Sur la prairie bleue et verte
Où vont chevaux et perdreaux
Sur la plaine blanche et noire
Où vont corbeaux et renards
Voir clair dans le chant des crapauds
Dans le désordre des insectes
Dans les astres de la rosée
Dans les astres des oeufs couvés
Dans la chaleur réglée et pure
Dans le vent dur du vieil hiver
Dans un monde mort et vivant

II

Le poids d'un chien sortant de l'eau
Comme un sourire ému d'une brouille d'amis
Miroirs brisés miroirs entiers

Le poids toujours nouveau
D'une chatte duvet
Les griffes sous la mousse

Et le poids flamboyant
D'une chatte écorchée
Par un fourreau d'aiguilles

Le poids du jour qui réfléchit
Et qui s'arrête comme un âne
A chaque pas

Et je ramasse avec lui
Les miettes de son effort
Sempiternel

Uninterrupted poetry [1946]

Familiar natural world

To see clearly and recognize
On the blue and green prairie
Where horses and partridges go
On the white and black plain
Where crows and foxes go
To see clearly into the toads' song
In the disorder of insects
In the stars of the dew
In the stars of incubating eggs
In the regulated pure warmth
In the hard wind of old winter
In a world dead and alive

II

The weight of a dog coming out of the water
Like a telling smile in a tangle of friends
Broken mirrors whole mirrors

The weight forever new
Of a downy cat
Claws under the moss

And the flamboyant weight
Of a feline scratched
By a coat of needles

The weight of a day that ponders
And balks like a donkey
At every step

And I gather up
The crumbs
Of its eternal effort

D'où sommes-nous sinon d'ici
Et d'ailleurs toujours en butte
À ce compte monotone
D'armées et de solitaires

Bain d'abeilles paravent
De la poussière immuable
Balance des hirondelles
Dans une poitrine vide

Âne chèvre jusqu'à l'herbe
Rat de la poupe à la proue
Rossignol jusqu'au déluge
Jusqu'aux étoiles éteintes

Sont pesants les rongeurs
Pesants comme une horloge
Et les poissons pêchés
Et l'hermine par sa blancheur
Et le lièvre par son repos

Je suis avec toutes les bêtes
Pour m'oublier parmi les hommes.

Uninterrupted poetry   [1946]

Where do we come from if not from right here
Moreover always harassed by
This monotonous account
Of armies and solitary people

A bath of bees a screen
Of unchangeable dust
A scales of swallows
In an empty breast

Donkey goat even the grass
Rat from poopdeck to prow
Nightingale as far as the flood
As far as the stars snuffed out

Heavy are the rodents
Heavy like a clock
And the fish that are caught
And the ermine by its whiteness
And the hare by its stillness

I am with the beasts
To forget myself among men.

À MARC CHAGALL

Âne ou vache coq ou cheval
Jusqu'à la peau d'un violon
Homme chanteur un seul oiseau
Danseur agile avec sa femme

Couple trempé dans son printemps

L'or de l'herbe le plomb du ciel
Séparés par les flammes bleues
De la santé de la rosée
Le sang s'irise le coeur tinte
Un couple le premier reflet

Et dans un souterrain de neige
La vigne opulente dessine
Un visage aux lèvres de lune
Qui n'a jamais dormi la nuit.

PAR UN BAISER

Jour la maison et nuit la rue
Les musiciens de la rue
Jouent tous à perte de silence
Sous le ciel noir nous voyons clair

La lampe est pleine de nos yeux
Nous habitons notre vallée
Nos murs nos fleurs notre soleil
Nos couleurs et notre lumière

La capitale du soleil
Est à l'image de nous-mêmes
Et dans l'asile de nos murs
Notre porte est celle des hommes.

The difficult desire to endure [1946]

TO MARC CHAGALL

Donkey or cow cock or horse
Even the skin of a violin
Man singer a single bird
Agile dancer with his woman

Couple immersed in their springtime

Gold of the grass leaden sky
Divided by blue flames
Of the dew's vitality
Blood is iridescent the heart rings out
A couple the first reflection

And in a snowy underground
The opulent vine draws
A face with lips of moon
That has never slept at night.

BY A KISS

Day the house and night the street
The street musicians
Dispel the silence playing
Under the black sky we see clearly

The lamp is full of our eyes
We dwell in our valley
Our walls our flowers our sunshine
Our colors and our light

The capital of the sun
Is in our own image
And within the retreat of our walls
Our door is a door for men.

255

Le dur désir de durer [1946]

SAISONS

I

Le centre du monde est partout et chez nous

Une rue s'offrit au soleil
Où était-elle et de quel poids
Dans la lumière suppliante
De l'hiver né du moindre amour

De l'hiver un enfant de rien
Avec sa suite de haillons
Avec son cortège de peurs
Et de pieds froids sur des tombeaux

Dans le doux désert de la rue.

II

Le centre du monde est partout et chez nous

Soudain la terre bienvenue
Fut une rose de fortune
Visible avec de blonds miroirs
Où tout chantait à rose ouverte

À verte feuille et blanc métal
Poisseux d'ivresse et de chaleur
Or oui de l'or pour naitre au sol
Sous l'écrasante multitude

Sous la vie accablante et bonne.

The difficult desire to endure   [1946]

SEASONS

I

The center of the world is all around and within us

A street is offered to the sunlight
Where was it and what did it weigh
In the suppliant light
Of winter born of the least love

Of the winter a child of nothing
With his following of rags
With his procession of fears
And cold feet on the tombstones

In the gentle desert of the street.

II

The center of the world is around and within us

Suddenly the welcome earth
Became a rose of fortune
Visible with milky mirrors
The whole world singing like a rose in bloom

On green leaf and white metal
Pitchy with drink and heat
Golden yes golden to be born in the ground
Under the crushing multitude

Under life overwhelming and good.

NOTRE VIE

Nous n'irons pas au but un par un mais par deux
Nous connaissant par deux nous nous connaîtrons tous
Nous nous aimerons tous et nos enfants riront
De la légende noire où pleure un solitaire.

OUR LIFE

We won't go one by one to our destiny but by twos
Knowing each other by twos we will all know one other
We shall be friends and our children will laugh at
The black legend [1] where a lonely man weeps.

---

[1] The "Black legend" often refers to the abuses of Latin American natives by the conquistadors, suggesting later wars of dominion in the twentieth century. Eluard weeps for the terrible loss of lives in these wars, as well as for the loss of his second wife Nusch in 1946.

"LA POÉSIE DOIT AVOIR POUR BUT LA VÉRITÉ PRATIQUE"

À mes amis exigeants

Si je vous dis que le soleil dans la forêt
Est comme un ventre qui se donne dans un lit
Vous me croyez vous approvez tous mes désirs

Si je vous dis que le cristal d'un jour de pluie
Sonne toujours dans la paresse de l'amour
Vous me croyez vous allongez le temps d'aimer

Si je vous dis que sur les branches de mon lit
Fait son nid un oiseau qui ne dit jamais oui
Vous me croyez vous partagez mon inquiétude

Si je vous dis que dans le golfe d'une source
Tourne la clé d'un fleuve entr'ouvrant la verdure
Vous me croyez encore plus vous comprenez

Mais si je chante sans détours ma rue entière
Et mon pays entier comme une rue sans fin
Vous me croyez plus vous allez au désert

Car vous marchez sans but sans savoir que les hommes
Ont besoin d'être unis d'espérer de lutter
Pour expliquer le monde et pour le transformer

D'un seul pas de mon coeur je vous entrainerai
Je suis sans forces j'ai vécu je vis encore
Mais je m'étonne de parler pour vous ravir
Quand je voudrais vous libérer pour vous confondre
Aussi bien avec l'algue et le jonc de l'aurore
Qu'avec nos frères qui construisent leur lumière.

Two poets of today[1] *[1947]*

"POETRY MUST HAVE PRACTICAL TRUTH AS ITS GOAL"

To my exacting friends

If I tell you that the sun in the forest
Is like a fecund body in bed
You believe me you approve all my desires

If I tell you that the crystal of a rainy day
Rings with the lassitude of love
You believe me you extend the time for loving

If I tell you that a bird that never says yes
Is building its nest on the branches of my bed
You believe me you share my concern

If I tell you that in a spring's well
The river key turns opening to verdure
You believe me you even understand

But if I sing of my whole street without detours
And of my whole country like an endless street
You believe me you even go to the desert

You have no destination unaware that men
Must be together to hope to struggle
To explain the world and transform it

With a single heartbeat I will take you along
I've little strength I have lived I'm still alive
But I am surprised to be speaking to delight you
I would rather free you to bring you together
As much with algae and the reeds of dawn
As with our brothers building their light.

---

[1] Eluard and Aragon refused to include these poems in *Poètes d'Aujourd'hui*, an anthology coedited by Jean Paulhan, when he proposed that writers "on the black list" for collaborating with the Nazis be pardoned for their errors.

À RENÉ MAGRITTE

Les yeux et les seins nus
Un sourire sur le lit
S'était étendu

La lumière les bras levés
A sa toilette
La lumière faisait le point
De sa beauté

Sous le lit une valse
Sur le pont d'un navire
Danse de cale basse

Le ciel remue se convertit répare
Lumière épouse une chair éternelle
Et le soleil a la chair ferme et rose
Sourire est peu il lui faut rire un brin

Rien n'est réel que ce rire en parade
Coeur sans respect à l'aise dans ses draps
Rire a la main plus lourde qu'un fruit mùr

Et les malheurs terrestres sont jugés.

To see [1948]

TO RENÉ MAGRITTE[1]

Eyes and bare breasts
A smile had stretched out
On the bed

Light her arms raised
At the dressing table
Light accentuated
Her beauty

Under the bed a waltz
On the ship's deck
The dance of the lower hold

The sky stirs is transformed then restored
Light weds an eternal flesh
The sun has firm rosy flesh
Smiling isn't much she needs to laugh a bit

Nothing is so real as this laughter parading
Disrespectful heart lolling in its sheets
Mockery is heavier-handed than a ripe fruit

And our earthly troubles are judged.

---

[1] Belgian surrealist painter who illustrated Eluard's *Les nécessités de la vie
et les conséquences des rêves*. Magritte's works depict fanciful, impossible
situations (violins embraced by snakes, etc.)

263

DE L'HORIZON D'UN HOMME À L'HORIZON DE TOUS

Après le plus grand abandon, quand il n'eut plus au fond de lui-même que la vision de sa femme morte, il fut secoué d'une grande révolte.

À MES CAMARADES IMPRIMEURS

Nous avions le même métier
Qui donnait à voir dans la nuit
Voir c'est comprendre c'est agir
Et voir c'est être ou disparaître

Il fallait y croire il fallait
Croire que l'homme a le pouvoir
D'être libre d'être meilleur
Que le destin qui lui est fait

Nous attendions un grand printemps
Nous attendions la vie parfaite
Et que la clarté se décide
À porter tout le poids du monde.

EN ESPAGNE

S'il y a en Espagne un arbre teint de sang
C'est l'arbre de la liberté

S'il y a en Espagne une bouche bavarde
Elle parle de liberté

S'il y a en Espagne un verre de vin pur
C'est le peuple qui le boira.

Political poems [1948]

FROM THE HORIZON OF ONE TO THE HORIZON OF ALL

After the greatest abandon, when he had nothing left within himself
but the vision of his deceased wife, he was shaken by a great revolt.

TO MY COMRADES THE PRINTERS

We had the same trade
That helped others to see in the night
Seeing is understanding is acting
Seeing is being or disappearing

We had to believe in that
Believe that people have the power
To be free to be better
Than their allotted destiny

We were waiting for a great springtime
We were waiting for the perfect life
And for light to decide to carry
The whole weight of the world.

IN SPAIN

If there is one bloodstained tree in Spain
It is the tree of liberty[1]

If there is one garrulous mouth in Spain
It speaks of liberty

If there is a glass of pure wine in Spain
It is the people who will drink it.

---

[1] Figuratively or specifically, the ancient oak "tree of liberty" in Guernica.

DES JOURS ENTRE LES JOURS
DES HOMMES ENTRE LES HOMMES

Apportez tout ce qui vit sur leur tombe
Non seulement des fleurs mais votre espoir
Tout ce qui vit à la lumière de l'espoir
Vos mains et votre chair et votre vue du monde
Immense sans remords sans regrets innocente
Votre coeur qui bat près d'un autre coeur
Apportez tout cela sur cette dérision
Qu'est une tombe ô souvenir fils de la vie

Nous n'avons pas le culte de la mort
Nous haissons la mort il nous faut peu de chose
Pour accepter la vie meme quand elle est lourde
Sous n'importe quel ciel la mort a peu de sens
Ils étaient comme nous écoutons leur passé
Il est en nous ils sont vivants dans notre espoir
Ils ont eu simplement la force de combattre
Pour vivre et nous nous combattons

Pour assurer leur vie en nous contre la mort.

VENCER JUNTOS

Ici la vie est limitée
Par cette ligne de sang noir
Qui nous sépare
Des prisons et des tombeaux

Ici nous sommes rabaissés
Par le supplice de l'Espagne
Ici la vie est menacée
Par la frontière de l'Espagne

Mais que l'Espagne crie victoire
Et notre sang deviendra chair
Chair confondue et chair heureuse
La France aura gagné sa guerre.

OF DAYS AMONG DAYS
OF MEN AMONG MEN

Bring everything alive to their tombs
Not just flowers but your hope
Everything that lives in the light of hope
Your hands and flesh your view of this immense world
Remorseless innocent without regrets
Your heart beating near another heart
Bring all that to heap on this derision
Of a tomb to remember life's children

We do not adhere to the cult of death
Death is hateful it takes so little for us
To accept life even as it weighs upon us
Under any sky death has little sense
They were like us let us listen to their past
It is a part of us they are alive in our hope
They simply had the strength to fight
In order to live and we go on fighting

To assure their lives in ours against death.

TO WIN TOGETHER

Here life is limited
By that line of black blood
That separates us
From prisons and graves

Here we are demeaned
By the anguish of Spain
Here life is threatened
By the frontier of Spain

But let Spain cry victory
And our blood will become
Flesh united and happy
France will have won its war.

DIT DE LA FORCE DE L'AMOUR

Entre tous mes tourments entre la mort et moi
Entre mon désespoir et la raison de vivre
Il y a l'injustice et ce malheur des hommes
Que je ne peux admettre il y a ma colère

Il y a les maquis couleur de sang d'Espagne
Il y a les maquis couleur du ciel de Grèce
Le pain le sang le ciel et le droit à l'espoir
Pour tous les innocents qui haïssent le mal

La lumière toujours est tout près de s'éteindre
La vie toujours s'apprête à devenir fumier
Mais le printemps renaît qui n'en a pas fini
Un bourgeon sort du noir et la chaleur s'installe

Et la chaleur aura raison des égoistes
Leurs sens atrophiés n'y résisteront pas
J'entends le feu parler en riant de tiédeur
J'entends un homme dire qu'il n'a pas souffert

Toi qui fus de ma chair la conscience sensible
Toi que j'aime à jamais toi qui m'as inventé
Tu ne supportais pas l'oppression ni l'injure
Tu chantais en rêvant le bonheur sur la terre

Tu rêvais d'être libre et je te continue.

SONG OF THE FORCE OF LOVE

With all my torments between myself and death
Between my despair and the reason for living
There is injustice and this misery of men
I cannot accept there is my anger

There are the maquis[1] the color of Spanish blood
There are the maquis the color of the Grecian sky
Bread and blood the sky and the right to hope
For all the innocents who abhor evil

Light is always ready to fade
Life is always preparing to rot
But spring is reborn not having done with it
A bud emerges from the dark and warmth settles in

Warmth will have the last word over the egoists
Their atrophied senses will not resist it
I hear the fire chattering laughing with warmth
I hear a man say he hasn't suffered

You who were the sensitive conscience of my flesh
You whom I love forever you who invented me
You would not tolerate oppression nor insult
You sang dreaming of happiness on earth

You dreamed of being free and I continue you.[2]

---

[1] The *maquis* (Italian: *macchia*) is the dense scrub vegetation of Mediterranean countries where Resistance fighters often joined forces in hiding from troops of the occupation. By extension, the term may also refer to a group of these fighters.
[2] He addresses the memory of Nusch, who died in 1946.

DANS VARSOVIE LA VILLE FANTASTIQUE

Qui n'a pas vu les ruines du Ghetto
Ne connaît pas le destin de son corps
Quand mort le fête et que son coeur pourrit
Quand son unique absence fait le vide

Pour qui a vu les ruines du Ghetto
Les faits humains ne sont pas à refaire
Tout doit changer sinon la mort s'installe
Mort est à vaincre ou bien c'est le désert

Or c'est ici que se montre le monstre
Fier de sortir du coeur même de l'homme
De l'homme enchaîné de l'homme rompu
Qui ne voit plus clair qui ne pense plus

Le Ghetto mort son ombre est sous le monstre
Mais son courage fut d'amours communes
D'amours passées qui renaîtront futures
Nouées fleuries de tête et de racines

Et sous le ciel ployant de Varsovie
La longue peine et la souffrance insigne
Défont refont un rêve de bonheur
L'espoir compose un arc-en-ciel de routes

L'homme en terre fait place à l'homme sur la terre.

IN WARSAW THE FANTASTIC CITY

Whoever has not seen the ruins of the Ghetto[1]
Does not know its body's destiny
When death claims it and its heart rots
When its unique absence creates a void

For one who has seen the ruins of the Ghetto
Such human acts are not to be repeated
It must all change or death takes over
Such death must be overcome or this is the desert

Here now the monster shows his face
Proud of emerging from the very heart of man
Man chained man broken who
No longer sees clearly no longer thinks

The Ghetto dead its shadow is under the monster
Its courage was made of common loves
Of past loves that will be reborn
Knotted flowering from the head and roots

And under the bowed sky of Warsaw
The long and inconceivable suffering
Undo and remake a dream of happiness
Hope builds a rainbow of pathways

Man interred gives way to man on earth.

---

[1] Jews living elsewhere in Poland were relocated to the Ghettos of Lodz and Warsaw, thriving communities before the German occupation, before being deported to concentration camps. Only a few had miraculously survived at the time of the Polish liberation. Two interpretations of the French poem are possible; the first speaks of the death of the Ghetto; the second translates "son corps" as "his body" referring to the one who cannot imagine the reality of his own inevitable death, not having seen the destruction of that place.

Poèmes politiques [1948]

DE PREMIER MAI EN PREMIER MAI

Comme si nous étions les feuilles d'un même arbre
Nous sommes rassemblés par le vent étouffant
Misère c'est la nuit et guerre le déluge
Du miroir qu'on nous tend ne reste que le plomb

Et ce n'est pas d'hier mais de toujours qu'on ose
Nous promettre au néant nous qui rajeunissons
A chaque bon baiser comme à chaque printemps
Nous qui puisons dans l'avenir notre lumière

D'un ciel mal étalé nos maîtres sont marqués
Nous notre force est nue elle est une et première
Toujours et pour demain sur terre nous les hommes
Nous ne connaîtrons plus que le poids du bonheur

Le poids léger et doux des bourgeons et des fruits.

SOEURS D'ESPÉRANCE

Soeurs d'espérance ô femmes courageuses
Contre la mort vous avez fait un pacte
Celui d'unir les vertus de l'amour

O mes soeurs survivantes
Vous jouez votre vie
Pour que la vie triomphe

Le jour est proche ô mes soeurs de grandeur
Où nous rirons des mots guerre et misère
Rien ne tiendra de ce qui fut douleur

Chaque visage aura droit aux caresses.

FROM MAY FIRST TO MAY FIRST

As if we were the leaves of the same tree
We are gathered together by the stifling wind
Misery is the night and war the deluge
From the mirror they hold before us only the lead remains

It's not just from yesterday but forever that they dare
To promise us to oblivion we who grow younger
With each good kiss just as with each springtime
We who press our light into the future

From a poorly displayed sky our masters are marked
Our strength is apparent it is one and foremost
Always and for tomorrow on earth we humans
Will know only the weight of happiness

The sweet light weight of buds and fruits.

SISTERS OF HOPE

Sisters of hope courageous women
You have made a pact against death
To unite the virtues of love

Oh my surviving sisters
You gamble your lives
So that life may triumph

The day is near my worthy sisters
When we will laugh about the words war and misery
Nothing will remain of our suffering

Every face will have a right to be caressed.

POUVOIR TOUT DIRE

Le tout est de tout dire et je manque de mots
Et je manque de temps et je manque d'audace
Je rêve et je dévide au hasard mes images
J'ai mal vécu et mal appris à parler clair

Tout dire les rochers la route et les pavés
Les rues et leurs passants les champs et les bergers
Le duvet du printemps la rouille de l'hiver
Le froid et la chaleur composant un seul fruit

Je veux montrer la foule et chaque homme en détail
Avec ce qui l'anime et qui le désespère
Et sous ses saisons d'homme tout ce qu'il éclaire
Son espoir et son sang son histoire et sa peine

Je veux montrer la foule immense divisée
La foule cloisonnée comme en un cimetière
Et la foule plus forte que son ombre impure
Ayant rompu ses murs ayant vaincu ses maîtres

La famille des mains la famille des feuilles
Et l'animal errant sans personnalité
Le fleuve et la rosée fécondants et fertiles
La justice debout le bonheur bien planté

Le bonheur d'un enfant saurai-je le déduire
De sa poupée ou de sa balle ou du beau temps
Et le bonheur d'un homme aurai-je la vaillance
De le dire selon sa femme et ses enfants

Saurai-je mettre au clair l'amour et ses raisons
Sa tragédie de plomb sa comédie de paille
Les actes machinaux qui le font quotidien
Et les caresses qui le rendent éternel

TO BE ABLE TO TELL IT ALL

I must tell it all yet words fail me
I haven't enough time and I dare not
I dream and spin off my images at random
I have not lived well nor learned to say what I mean

To tell it all the rocks the road the cobblestones
The streets and their passersby the fields and the shepherds
The down of spring the decay of winter
Cold and warmth composing a single fruit

I want to show the crowd and each man in detail
With what delights him and leads him to despair
Everything he brightens in the seasons of a lifetime
His hope and his blood his story and his suffering

I want to show the great divided population
The crowd partitioned as in a cemetery
And the crowd stronger than its impure shadow
Having broken down its walls and overcome the masters[1]

The family of hands the family of leaves
And the wandering animal without distinction
The river and the morning dew fecund and fertile
Justice standing happiness well grounded

Will I know how to deduce a child's happiness
From her doll or her ball or a beautiful day
Will I have the courage to tell a man's happiness
As his wife and children see it

Will I be able to throw light on the reasons for love
Its leaden tragedy its straw comedy
The routines that make it commonplace
And the caresses that make it eternal

---

[1]"The masters" are the dictators and those who carry out their work.

Pouvoir tout dire [1951]

Et pourrai-je jamais enchaîner la récolte
À l'engrais comme on fait du bien à la beauté
Pourrai-je comparer le besoin au désir
Et l'ordre mécanique à l'ordre du plaisir

Aurai-je assez de mots pour liquider la haine
Par la haine sous l'aile énorme des colères
Et montrer la victime écraser les bourreaux
Saurai-je colorer le mot révolution

L'or libre de l'aurore en des yeux sûrs d'eux-mêmes
Rien n'est semblable tout est neuf tout est précieux
J'entends de petits mots devenir des adages
L'intelligence est simple au-delà des souffrances

Contre saurai-je dire à quel point je suis contre
Les absurdes manies que noue la solitude
J'ai failli en mourir sans pouvoir me défendre
Comme en meurt un héros ligoté bâillonné

J'ai failli en être dessous corps coeur esprit
Sans formes et aussi avec toutes les formes
Dont on entoure pourriture et déchéance
Et complaisance et guerre indifférence et crime

Il s'en fallut de peu que mes frères
Je m'affirmais sans rien comprendre à leur combat
Je croyais prendre au présent plus qu'il ne possède
Mais je n'avais aucune idée du lendemain

Contre la fin de tout je dois ce que je suis
Aux hommes qui ont su ce que la vie contient
A tous les insurgés vérifiant leurs outils
Et vérifiant leur coeur et se serrant la main

To be able to tell it all *[1951]*

Will I ever be able to link the harvest
To the soil enriched just as beauty grows with love
Can I compare the need to the desire
And mechanical order to the order of pleasure

Will I have enough words to destroy hate
With hate under the vast wing of anger
And point out the victim crush the hangmen
Will I know how to color the word revolution

The free gold of dawn in confident eyes
Nothing is the same all is new and precious
I hear small words becoming adages
Intelligence beyond suffering is easy

Will I know how to say how much I am against
The absurd manias knotted by solitude
I almost died of them unable to defend myself
Like a hero bound and gagged

I barely escaped dissolution of body heart and mind
Formless yet with all the forms
Common to rot and desuetude
Complacency and war indifference and crime

It wouldn't have taken much for my brothers to reject me
I affirmed my position without understanding their struggle
I thought I could take more from the present than it holds
Without thinking of the next day

Against obliteration I owe what I am
To those who knew what life holds
To all the insurgents checking out their tools
Confirming their good will in a handclasp

Pouvoir tout dire [1951]

Hommes continuement entre humains sans un pli
Un chant monte qui dit ce que toujours ont dit
Ceux qui dressaient notre avenir contre la mort
Contre les souterrains des nains et des déments

Pourrai-je dire enfin la porte s'est ouverte
De la cave où les fûts mettaient leur masse sombre
Sur la vigne où le vin captive le soleil
En employant les mots du vigneron lui-même

Les femmes sont taillées comme l'eau ou la pierre
Tendres ou trop entières dures ou légères
Les oiseaux passent au travers d'autres espaces
Un chien familier traine en quête d'un vieil os

Minuit n'a plus d'écho que pour un très vieil homme
Qui gâche son trésor en des chansons banales
Même cette heure de la nuit n'est pas perdue
Je ne m'endormirai que si d'autres s'éveillent

Pourrai-je dire rien ne vaut que la jeunesse
En montrant le sillon de l'âge sur la joue
Rien ne vaut que la suite infinie des reflets
A partir de l'élan des graines et des fleurs

A partir d'un mot franc et des choses réelles
La confiance ira sans idée de retour
Je veux que l'on réponde avant que l'on questionne
Et nul ne parlera une langue étrangère

To be able to tell it all [1951]

People shoulder to shoulder without a break
A song rises telling what those who were preparing our future
Have always said against death and
The devious ways of subhumans and madmen [1]

Can I say at last the door has opened to the cellar
Where mallets used to bear down on vines
Where the wine captures the sun
To use the winegrower's own words

Women are shaped like water or stone
Tender or too complete resistant or pliant
The birds pass through other spaces
A familiar dog lags behind looking for an old bone

Midnight echoes only for a very old man
Spoiling his treasure with common songs
Even this hour of the night is not lost
I shall sleep only if others awaken

Pointing to age that furrows my cheek
Can I say only youth is of value
Only the infinite succession of reflections
Beginning with the bursting of seeds and flowers

Beginning with an honest word and real things
Confidence will go forth without faltering
I want people to answer before they are questioned
And none will speak a foreign tongue

---

[1] A reference to the Nazis and collaborators in the subjugation of freedom
fighters worldwide.

Et nul n'aura envie de piétiner un toit
D'incendier des villes d'entasser des morts
Car j'aurai tous les mots qui servent à construire
Et qui font croire au temps comme à la seule source

Il faudra rire mais on rira de santé
On rira d'être fraternel à tout moment
On sera bon avec les autres comme on l'est
Avec soi-même quand on s'aime d'être aimé

Les frissons délicats feront place à la houle
De la joie d'exister plus fraîche que la mer
Plus rien ne nous fera douter de ce poème
Que j'écris aujourd'hui pour effacer hier.

To be able to tell it all [1951]

No one will want to trample our rooftops
Burn cities or pile up the dead
For I will have all the words for building
To believe in time as in the single source

We shall have to laugh but in good health
We shall laugh for being fraternal at every moment
We will be good to each other as to ourselves
When we like ourselves for being loved

Delicate shivers will give way to the groundswell
Of joy for being alive fresher than the sea
Nothing more can make us doubt this poem I write
Today to erase yesterday.

Pouvoir tout dire   [1951]

LE GRAND SOUCI DES HOMMES DE MON TEMPS

Au mal:

Rien qu'un homme se heurte au temps
Le mal l'absorbe en son naufrage

Et je parle déjà d'un temps révolu
D'un autre temps d'un ancien temps

Ses doutes dansent dans son sang
La joie l'accable
Le ciel rouge le ronge
Il unit dans son coeur le bois mort et la fleur
La mer est plutôt difficile
Et la terre est plutôt ingrate

Ses yeux s'injectent de sa graisse
Ou de sa faim de son envie
Ses yeux se heurtent aux carrefours
De l'amour de la haine
De la folie et du génie

Il est à la fois comme un roc
Dans la tempête et comme un coq
Dans la marmite
Comme un savant sur son tremplin
Comme un enfant sous sa fessée
Comme un homme incertain de soi-même demain

Comprenez-moi je veux vous donner à penser
Que tout n'a pas été si facile ni gai

Mémoire et prévoyance sont bien trop fragiles
Pour qu'il connaisse d'où il vient
Ni où il va

To be able to tell it all [1951]

THE GREAT WORRY OF THE MEN OF MY TIME

To evil:

Just let a man collide with time
Evil swallows him up in the wreckage

I am speaking now of a time gone by
A time of long ago

Doubts dance in his veins
Joy overwhelms him
A reddened sky gnaws at him
He joins in his heart dead wood and the flower
The sea is rather difficult
And the land is quite ungrateful

His eyes are injected with his fat
Or his hunger or his greed
His eyes bump into the crossroads
Of love and hate
Of madness and genius

He is at once a rock
In the storm and a cock
In the pot
Like a wiseman on his trampoline
Like a child being spanked
Like a man unsure of himself tomorrow

Understand me I want you to know
It's not all been easy or fun

Memory and foresight are much too fragile
For him to know where he comes from
Or where he's going

Pouvoir tout dire [1951]

Il chérit la justice amère
Et les vieilles vertus qui avaient fait le point
Entre richesse et pauvreté

Il sait qu'il doit avoir vingt ans
Et qu'il doit être vieux dans les moments qui suivent
Il sait qu'il ne passera pas
Comme passe le ciel sur toutes les récoltes
Pour se régénérer
Et ses lendemains sont aveugles

Il fait à peine jour dans son cerveau de plomb
Ses os sont de poussière et sa paume est la lune
Un tout petit espace un milliard de fois mort
La prudence a pour lui un poids définitif
Les maîtres de sa vie sont des bêtes obscures
Quand il s'endort il craint de ne pas s'éveiller

Hommes de l'avenir il vous faut voir hier
Je vous parle des morts qui sont morts sans printemps

Au bien:

Le solitaire allait de miroir en miroir
Pour peupler de son ombre le désert des soirs

Hommes de l'avenir je parle d'aujourd'hui
Je suis dans le présent je veux vous en convaincre

Je suis parmi la foule énorme des vivants
Elle a repris conscience
Au bout de ses millions de bras ses mains espèrent
Elle se nourrit d'elle-même
De son courage de son coeur
Elle s'alourdit de confiance

To be able to tell it all [1951]

He cherishes bitter justice
And the old virtues that distinguished
Between wealth and poverty

He knows he has to be twenty
And that later on he must be old
He knows he cannot go on
Like the sky that passes over all the harvests
Only to be renewed
And his tomorrows are blind

The rays of dawn barely penetrate his leaden brain
His bones are dust his palm is the moon
In a very short space he's died a billion deaths
Prudence has a definite weight for him
The masters of his life are obscure beasts
When he falls asleep he fears he may not waken

Men of tomorrow you must look at yesterday
I speak of those who died without a springtime

To the good:

The solitary man went from mirror to mirror looking
For his shadow to fill the deserted evenings

Men of tomorrow I speak of today
I want you to know I live today

I belong to the huge crowd of the living
That has regained consciousness
From millions of arms hands reach out in hope
The crowd is sustained
By its own courage and heart
It gains strength with trust

285

Pouvoir tout dire [1951]

Elle s'allège en travaillant
Et les longues minutes du travail fourmillent
Du bonheur de demain
De la faim de demain
Un appel d'air même les pierres fleuriront
Les yeux prendront naissance dans le flot des yeux

Il n'y a plus de solitaire
Il n'y a plus d'homme fardé de son propre mystère
Il y a sur le ciel d'aujourd'hui de demain
Des hommes couronnés de leur pensée commune
Amie comme est ami l'oiseau avec ses plumes
Amie comme est ami le drame avec ses larmes

Comprenez-moi tout devient compréhensible
Demain reste le centre de la vie totale

Bien sûr il y a eu des loques et des ruines
Des épines des déceptions
Des mains vides des fronts couverts de suie et de rancoeur
Il y a eu le crime et les supplices sans raison
Et le secret abominable de celui qui fait le mal
Il y a eu sans un baiser des bouches creuses des yeux vides

Mais nous avons aimé nos héros nos martyrs
Et nous les nommons nos seuls juges
Ils sont à la grandeur des plus hauts rêves de demain
Dans leur combat ils ont la couleur de l'éveil
Ils sortent de la mort tout habillés d'aurore
Ils sont nos frères renaissants et vigoureux

Ils ont refusé la misère
La misère qui tue avec de vieilles armes
La guerre leur est apparue comme une femme sans enfants

To be able to tell it all *[1951]*

It becomes lighthearted working
And the long minutes of work are buzzing
With tomorrow's happiness
With tomorrow's hunger
A cry for air even the stones will flower
Eyes will be born in the sea of eyes

No more is there a solitary man
Powdered over with his own mystery
On the horizons of today and tomorrow there are
Men crowned with their common thought
Like a friend as the bird is a friend to its feathers
As tragedy is a friend to its tears

Understand me everything becomes clear
Tomorrow remains the center of total life

To be sure there have been rags and ruins
Thorns and disappointments
Empty hands brows covered with sweat and resentment
There has been crime and torture without reason
The abominable secret of one who does wrong
There have been hollow mouths without a kiss and empty eyes

But we have loved our heroes our martyrs
We name them our sole judges
They are worthy of tomorrow's noblest dreams
In their struggle they are the color of waking
They rise from death all dressed in dawn
They are our brothers reborn vigorous
They refused misery
The misery that kills with old weapons
War appeared to them like a childless woman

Pouvoir tout dire [1951]

Sous le soleil et sur la terre ils ont voulu les hommes frères
Une guirlande sans un noeud de source en source

Et leurs sens étant clairs ils pressentaient le jour

Rien qu'un homme n'a plus de sens
Vivre est le seul refuge et la seule échappée.

Mexico, septembre 1949

To be able to tell it all [1951]

Under the sun and on earth they wanted men as brothers
A knotless garland from fountain to fountain
With keen senses they anticipated day

One man alone has no meaning
Living is the only refuge the only escape.

Mexico, September 1949

Pouvoir tout dire [1951]

LES POÈTES QUE J'AI CONNUS

Les poètes que j'ai connus
Leur souvenir comme l'automne
Multiplie le soleil dans l'ombre

Les poètes que j'ai connus
Vivants ou morts faibles ou forts
Les bienheureux les douloureux
Tous ceux que j'ai aimée compris
Pleins de défauts pleins de vertus
Ceux qui voulaient faire naufrage
Et ceux qui croyaient au salut

La masse de leur coeur changeait
Tantôt de cendres tantôt d'or
Leur parole était étendue

De plus en plus elle montait
Le long des lèvres de l'aurore
Sur les collines de candeur
Même quand le ciel était gris
Mais la voûte du ciel s'est brisée sur leur tête
Mais la source du charme s'est tarie dans l'herbe
Et les poètes sidérés ont répété l'appel aux armes
L'appel à la justice à la fraternité.

*

Et les poètes ont essayé
De se régler sur leurs semblables

Et j'arrive chez Aragon
Et j'entends Aragon parler
Me parler c'est-à-dire me montrer son coeur
Notre coeur

290

To be able to tell it all [1951]

THE POETS I HAVE KNOWN

The poets I have known
Their memory like the autumn
Multiplies the sun in the shadows

The poets I have known
Living or dead weak or strong
The fortunate the sorrowful
Including all those I have loved
Full of faults and virtues
Those who wanted to be shipwrecked
Those who believed in salvation

The mass of their heart would change
Sometimes ashes sometimes gold
Their word spread

More and more it rose
Along the lips of dawn
Over hills of candor
Even when the sky was grey
But the sky dome shattered over their heads
The source of charm dried up in the grass
And the dazed poets repeated the call to arms
The call to justice and fraternity.

                          *

And the poets tried to make amends
With their own kind

I go to see Aragon
I hear him talking to me
Baring his heart
Our heart

Pouvoir tout dire [1951]

"Il y a tant d'hommes sur terre
Bien plus sensibles que nous deux
Et tant d'yeux sombres et d'yeux bleus
Prompts à réduire tout mystère

Tant d'hommes clairs dans leur dessein
D'améliorer leur vie la vie
Que le soleil demain matin
Figurera leur énergie"

Avec mon ami Aragon les hommes savent s'exprimer
Dans leurs limites
Et au-delà de leurs limites
Dans leurs frontières
Et au-delà de leurs frontières

Le mot frontière est un mot borgne
L'homme a deux yeux pour voir le monde.

*

De tous les poètes que j'ai connus, Aragon est celui qui a eu le plus raison, raison contre les monstres — et raison contre moi.

Il m'a montré le droit chemin; il le montre encore aujourd'hui à tous ceux qui n'ont pas compris que lutter contre l'injustice, c'est lutter pour leur propre vie, pour une vie fleurie d'espoir et pour tout l'amour du monde.

Novembre 1949

292

To be able to tell it all   [1951]

"There are so many men on earth
Much more sensitive than the two of us
So many dark eyes and blue eyes
Ready to reduce all mystery

"So many clear in their purpose
To improve their lives and life itself
That tomorrow's sun
Will represent their energy"

With my friend Aragon men say what they mean
Within and beyond their limits
Within and beyond their frontiers

The word frontier is a one-eyed word
We have two eyes to see the world with.

*

Of all the poets I have known, Aragon[1] is the one who was
right, in opposing the monsters and in opposing me.

He showed me the right path; today he shows it to those who
did not understand that to fight against injustice is to fight for their
own lives, for a life flowering with hope and for the love of the whole
world.

November 1949

---

[1] Aragon, poet and novelist, was associated with the Surrealist movement
in the early days of their experimentation, breaking with them in 1930.
He was director of the Resistance fighters in the south of France during
the German Occupation of World War II.

Pouvoir tout dire   [1951]

AU JOUR

Mer et forêt montagne et plaine
Eau vivace feu bouillonnant
Joies et douleurs contradictions
Un autre verra clair pour moi.

*

Le soir l'ombre s'allonge
Jusqu'à un autre monde
Que nous nous partageons.

*

La lune et les eaux du fleuve
Et l'horizon de maisons
Plus vivace que ma chambre
La rosée et le soleil
Et la chaleur de mon coeur
Font avancer la vie et reculer la mort

Le temps ne sépare rien
L'éternité me rejoint.

LA LOI

Il y a toujours eu sur terre
Parmi la foule des visages
Un visage qui réduit
Un homme à sa descendance.

*

Presse-toi de penser à ton pays aux hommes
De ton pays aux frères des hommes par le monde
Ce sont d'anciens enfants ils tiennent leurs enfants
Sur leurs genoux et dans tous les pays
L'homme s'accorde avec l'enfant.

To be able to tell it all [1951]

IN THE LIGHT OF DAY

Sea and forest mountain and plain
Lively water boiling fire
Joys and sorrows contradictions
Another will see through it for me.

*

In the evening the shadow grows longer
Reaching another world
That we share with each other.

*

The moon and the river's waters
The horizon of houses
Livelier than my room
Morning dew and sunshine
And the warmth of my heart
Let life go forward death draw back
Time separates nothing

Eternity finds me again.

THE LAW

There has always been on earth
Among the crowd of faces
One face which reduces
A man to his ancestors.

*

Hurry up think of your country of the men
Of your country with brothers worldwide
Former children holding their own children
On their knees and in every country
Man is making peace with the child

Fais un enfant à l'image
De tes désirs de tes rêves
Presse-toi de penser à ton enfant qui court
Comme une fleur court du printemps à l'été
Du printemps au printemps de l'aurore à l'aurore

Rien ne vieillit les couleurs de la vie
Ne passent pas au grand soleil.

D'UN TEMPS FUTUR

Les prisons sont fermées aux prisonniers
Elles sont devenues des rochers dans la foule
J'en parle comme je respire
Si elles étaient ouvertes je serais dedans
Tout le monde est dehors.

*

Le travail est vivant
La fatigue est joyeuse
Je respire au-delà
De ma propre poitrine.

*

Les rues et les maisons les prés et les forêts
Brillent d'un même éclat chacun a son soleil
Les nuages sont dispersés
Il y a une foule de soleils dans l'air
Et l'amour est mutuel
Et l'émotion est générale

Je ne me souviens pas
Du passé désolant.

To be able to tell it all [1951]

Make a child in the image
Of your hopes and your dreams
Think of your child running
Like a flower from spring into summer
From spring to spring from dawn to dawn

Nothing grows old the colors of life
Do not fade in the great sun.

OF A FUTURE TIME

The prisons are closed to the prisoners
They have become old rocks in the crowd
I speak of them as I breathe
If they were open I would be inside
Everybody is outside.

                              *

Working is living
Fatigue is joyful
I breathe beyond
My own lungs.

                              *

Streets and houses fields and forests
Equally shine each has its sun
The clouds are dispersed
There's a crowd of suns in the air
And love is mutual
And emotion is general

I do not remember
The desolate past.

PÉTRIFICATION D'UN POÈTE
d'un poète commun

Il était doux comme laine
Et précieux comme soie
Ferma toutes ses fenêtres
Ferma les yeux pour se voir

Il se vit moins grand qu'un homme
Et plus grand que tous les dieux
Qu'il avait imaginés
Et qu'il savait illusoires

Son sang vivait sans chaleur
Sa tête était plus lointaine
Qu'une bulle de savon
Quand le soleil l'a happée

Alors il se sentit libre
Séparé des autres hommes
Alors il rentra sur terre
Comme un mort rentre sous terre.

EXALTATION D'UN POÈTE
de Vladimir Maiakovski

Il était doux comme laine
Et précieux comme soie
Il avait les mains plus faibles
Que des mains de jeune fille

To be able to tell it all [1951]

PETRIFICATION OF A POET
                    of an ordinary poet

He was soft as wool
Fine as silk
He closed all his windows
Closed his eyes to look within

He saw himself less than a man
And greater than all the gods
He had imagined
And knew to be illusory

His blood was living without warmth
His head was further off
Than a soap bubble
When the sun has snatched it up

Then he felt free
Apart from other men
Then he returned to earth
As a dead man goes back to the grave.

EXALTATION OF A POET
                    of Vladimir Maiakovski[1]

He was soft as wool
Fine as silk
With hands more delicate
Than a young girl's

---

[1] Russian futurist poet and dramatist, innovator of a free verse style, promoted the poster propaganda for the Bolshevik revolution, spent time in prison, and died at the age of 36 in 1930.

Savait parler aux enfants
Savait parler aux bonshommes
Il reflétait l'innocence
Mieux qu'une mère enfantine

Il avait les yeux capables
De voir ce que nul ne voit
Les enfers de la fatigue
La poussière de la mort

Il reflétait la science
Et l'ambition du travail
Et les détails du combat
Tel que l'espoir le conduit

Il clamait comme un canon
Les victoires de son peuple
Il ébouriffait la vie
Puis la coiffait par en haut

Dans l'ombre et sur la montagne
Sa justice était debout
Il savait pleurer et rire
Devant toutes les images

Dompteur expert en caresses
Ses colères ont fait peur
Alors il offrit sa chair
Au feu de ses ennemis

Et ses ennemis périrent
Et lui demeura vivant
Au coeur des plus simples gens
Son sang n'a plus fait qu'un tour

Le tour de l'humanité.

To be able to tell it all [1951]

He could talk to children
And to simple folk
With an air of innocence
Better than a childlike mother

His eyes were capable of seeing
What no one else could see
The hells of fatigue
The dust of death

He reflected science
The ambition of work
The details of combat
As hope directs it

The victories of his people
He declaimed like a cannon
He disheveled life
Then coiffed it from above

In the shadow and on the mountain
His justice stood tall
He could weep and laugh with joy
Before all images

A conqueror expert in carresses
His angry explosions were frightening
Then he offered his flesh
To the enemy fire

And his enemies perished
While he remained alive
In the hearts of the simplest people
His blood made only one more sally

Traveling the path of humanity.

Pouvoir tout dire [1951]

BONNE JUSTICE

C'est la chaude loi des hommes
Du raisin ils font du vin
Du charbon ils font du feu
Des baisers ils font des hommes

C'est la dure loi des hommes
Se garder intact malgré
Les guerres et la misère
Malgré les dangers de mort

C'est la douce loi des hommes
De changer l'eau en lumière
Le rêve en réalité
Et les ennemis en frères

Une loi vieille et nouvelle
Qui va se perfectionnant
Du fond du coeur de l'enfant
Jusqu'à la raison suprème.

To be able to tell it all [1951]

GOOD JUSTICE

It is the impelling law of men
From the grape they make wine
From coal they make fire
From embraces they make men

It is the harsh law of men
They must stay together
Despite wars and misery
And the dangers of death

It is the gentle law of men
To change water into light
Dreams into reality
To make brothers of our enemies

It's an old law and a new law
Which continues growing
From the bottom of a child's heart
Unto ultimate reason.

MENACES À LA VICTOIRE

Prends garde le miroir de la vie s'obscurcit

Le premier pas du sang une goutte de sang
Et la marche finale de la guerre et du sang
Du feu de la terreur des ruines du désert
La fin de l'homme sans raison
La fin de l'homme raisonnable
La mort la fin de la misère
La fin de l'oppression

Mais aussi la fin du possible.

*

Il ne faut pas périr mais vivre

Sur les traces des pas d'un couple
L'herbe pousse les fleurs s'inscrivent
Et partout où passent les hommes
On sent le printemps dans l'hiver
La rouille fond dans un baiser
La foule est une foule heureuse
Les enfants sont tout l'horizon

La paix rajeunira les hommes

*

Nous ne songerons plus jamais à prendre garde
Printemps été pluie et soleil
Automne reposant hiver espoir violent
Et sur toute frontière
De l'espace et du temps
Rien que des hommes fraternels
Rien que la même aurore et le même couchant
Printemps été automne hiver

L'écho et le reflet de la vie infinie.

To be able to tell it all [1951]

THREATS TO VICTORY

Watch out the mirror of life grows dark

The first trace of blood a drop of blood
The final march of war and of blood
Of the fire of terror ruins of the desert
The end of unreasonable man
The end of reasonable man
Death the end of misery
The end of oppression

But also the end of the possible.

*

We must not perish but live

On the traces of the footsteps of a couple
Grass grows flowers are inscribed
And whenever people pass
They smell springtime in the winter air
The rot crumbles away with a kiss
The crowd is a happy crowd
The children are the whole horizon

Peace will make us young again

*

Never again will we think of being on guard
Spring   summer   rain and sun
Restful autumn   winter   violent hope
And on every frontier
Of space and time
Only brothers and sisters sharing
The same dawn and the same sunset
Spring   summer   autumn   winter

The echo and reflection of infinite life.

305

LE VISAGE DE LA PAIX

1

Je connais tous les lieux où la colombe loge
Et le plus naturel est la tête de l'homme.

2

L'amour de la justice et de la liberté
A produit un fruit merveilleux
Un fruit qui ne se gâte point
Car il a le goût du bonheur.

3

Que la terre produise que la terre fleurisse
Que la chair et le sang vivants
Ne soient jamais sacrifiés.

4

Que le visage humain connaisse
L'utilité de la beauté
Sous l'aile de la réflexion.

5

Pour tous du pain pour tous des roses
Nous avons tous prêté serment
Nous marchons à pas de géant
La route n'est pas si longue.

The face of peace   [1951]

THE FACE OF PEACE[1]

1

I know all the places where the dove dwells
The most natural is in man's head.

2

The love of justice and liberty
Has produced a wonderful fruit
That never spoils
For it has the taste of happiness.

3

Let the earth produce and flower
Let flesh and blood
Never again be sacrificed.

4

Let human eyes perceive
The use of beauty
Under the wing of contemplation.

5

Bread and roses for everyone
We have all made a promise
We are taking giant steps
It's not such a long way to go.

---

[1] *Visage de la paix* was published with 29 illustrations by Picasso dated 5-XII-50, with the dove and the face of Françoise Gilot in multiple variations, to represent the face of peace.

6

Nous fuirons le repos nous fuirons le sommeil
Nous prendrons de vitesse l'aube et le printemps
Et nous préparerons des jours et des saisons
A la mesure de nos rêves.

7

La blanche illumination
De croire tout le bien possible.

8

L'homme en proie à la paix se couronne d'espoir.

9

L'homme en proie à la paix a toujours un sourire
Après tous les combats pour qui le lui demande.

10

Feu fertile des graines des mains et des paroles
Un feu de joie s'allume et chaque coeur a chaud

11

Vaincre s'appuie sur la fraternité

12

Grandir est sans limites

13

Chacun sera vainqueur

14

La sagesse pend au plafond
Et son regard tombe du front comme une lampe de cristal.

6

We shall neither rest nor sleep
We hasten to meet dawn and springtime
We shall prepare days and seasons
To the measure of our dreams.

7

The white illumination
Of believing good things can happen.

8

One caught up with peace is crowned with hope.

9

After the struggle one who is prey to peace
Has a ready smile for those who ask him for it.

10

Fertile of seeds of hands and words
A fire of joy lights up warming every heart.

11

Victory depends on brotherhood.

12

Growing has no limits.

13

Each shall overcome.

14

Wisdom hangs from the ceiling
Its glance hangs from the brow like a crystal lamp

15

La lumière descend lentement sur la terre
Du front le plus ancien elle passe au sourire
Des enfants délivrés de la crainte des chaînes.

16

Dire que si longtemps l'homme a fait peur à l'homme
Et fait peur aux oiseaux qu'il portait dans sa tête.

17

Après avoir lavé son visage au soleil
L'homme a besoin de vivre
Besoin de faire vivre et il s'unit d'amour
S'unit à l'avenir.

18

Mon bonheur c'est notre bonheur
Mon soleil c'est notre soleil
Nous nous partageons la vie
L'espace et le temps sont à tous.

19

L'amour est au travail il est infatigable.

20

C'était en mil neuf cent dix sept
Et nous gardons l'intelligence
De notre délivrance.

21

Nous avons inventé autrui
Comme autrui nous a inventé
Nous avions besoin l'un de l'autre.

15

Light falls slowly over the land
From the brow of the elder it passed to the smile
Of children delivered from the fear of bondage.

16

To think that for so long man has frightened man
He even frightened the winged ones
He carried in his head.

17

After washing our faces in the sun
We need to live
To help others live we join together with love
We join the future.

18

My happiness is our happiness
My sun is our sun
We share life space and time
Belong to everyone.

19

Love is at work
Indefatigable.

20

It was nineteen hundred and seventeen
We understand the importance
Of our liberation.

21

We invented others
As others invented us
We needed each other.

22

Comme un oiseau volant a confiance en ses ailes
Nous savons où nous mène notre main tendue
Vers notre frère

23

Nous allons combler l'innocence
De la force qui si longtemps
Nous a manqué
Nous ne serons jamais plus seuls

24

Nos chansons appellent la paix
Et nos réponses sont des actes pour la paix.

25

Ce n'est pas le naufrage c'est notre désir
Qui est fatal et c'est la paix qui est inévitable.

26

L'architecture de la paix
Repose sur le monde entier.

22

Just as a bird in flight believes in its wings
So we know where a hand reaching out
To our brother will lead us.

23

We shall crown innocence
With the resolve we lacked so long
We will never be alone again.

24

Our songs are calling for peace
Our answers are acts for peace.

25

It is not drowning but our desire
That is fatal and peace that is inevitable.

26

The architecture of peace
Rests on the whole world.

Le phénix [1951]

> *Le Phénix, c'est le couple—Adam et Eve—*
> *qui est et n'est pas le premier.*

LE PHÉNIX

Je suis le dernier sur ta route
Le dernier printemps la dernière neige
Le dernier combat pour ne pas mourir
Et nous voici plus bas et plus haut que jamais.

*

Il y a de tout dans notre bûcher
Des pommes de pin des sarments
Mais aussi des fleurs plus fortes que l'eau
De la boue et de la rosée.

*

La flamme est sous nos pieds la flamme nous couronne
A nos pieds des insectes des oiseaux des hommes
Vont s'envoler
Ceux qui volent vont se poser.

*

Le ciel est clair la terre est sombre
Mais la fumée s'en va au ciel
Le ciel a perdu tous ses feux
La flamme est restée sur la terre.

*

La flamme est la nuée du coeur
Et toutes les branches du sang
Elle chante notre air
Elle dissipe la buée de notre hiver.

314

The phoenix¹ [1951]

> *The Phoenix is the couple--Adam and Eve--
> the first couple, yet not the first.*

THE PHOENIX¹

I am the last one on your path
The last spring the last snow
The last struggle not to die

Here we are lower yet higher than ever.

*

There is everything in our woodshed
Pinecones woodbine
And flowers stronger than the water

Of mud and of dew.

*

Flame is under our feet and flame crowns us
Insects at our feet birds men
Will fly away

Those who fly will alight again.

*

The sky is clear the earth is dark
But smoke rises to the sky
The sky has lost all its fires

The flame remains on earth.

*

The flame is the cloud of the heart
And all the branches of the blood
It sings our tune

It dissipates the moist breath of our winter.

---

¹ These poems are for Dominique, whom Eluard met at a world peace
conference in Mexico, September, 1949, and married in 1951.

Le phénix [1951]

*

Nocturne et en horreur a flambé le chagrin
Les cendres ont fleuri en joie et en beauté
Nous tournons toujours le dos au couchant

Tout a la couleur de l'aurore.

PRINTEMPS

Il y a sur la plage quelques flaques d'eau
Il y a dans les bois des arbres fous d'oiseaux
La neige fond dans la montagne
Les branches des pommiers brillent de tant de fleurs
Que le pâle soleil recule

C'est par un soir d'hiver dans un monde très dur
Que je vis ce printemps près de toi l'innocente
Il n'y a pas de nuit pour nous
Rien de ce qui périt n'a de prise sur toi
Et tu ne veux pas avoir froid

Notre printemps est un printemps qui a raison.

The phoenix[1] *[1951]*

*

Nocturnal and in horror grief caught fire
The cinders flowered in joy and beauty
We always turn away from the setting sun

Everything is the color of dawn.

SPRING

There are pools of water on the beach
The trees in the woods are crazy with birds
Snow is melting on the mountain
The apple tree's branches shine with so many flowers
The pale sun draws back

It was on a winter evening in a hard world
I saw this spring near you, so innocent
There is no night for us
Nothing that perishes has a hold on you
And you don't want to be cold

Our springtime is a springtime that is right.

JE T'AIME

Je t'aime pour toutes les femmes que je n'ai pas connues
Je t'aime pour tous les temps où je n'ai pas vécu
Pour l'odeur du grand large et l'odeur du pain chaud
Pour la neige qui fond pour les premières fleurs
Pour les animaux purs que l'homme n'effraie pas
Je t'aime pour aimer
Je t'aime pour toutes les femmes que je n'aime pas

Qui me reflète sinon toi moi-même je me vois si peu
Sans toi je ne vois rien qu'une étendue déserte
Entre autrefois et aujourd'hui
Il y a eu toutes ces morts que j'ai franchies sur de la paille
Je n'ai pas pu percer le mur de mon miroir
Il m'a fallu apprendre mot par mot la vie
Comme on oublie

Je t'aime pour ta sagesse qui n'est pas la mienne
Pour la santé
Je t'aime contre tout ce qui n'est qu'illusion
Pour ce coeur immortel que je ne détiens pas
Tu crois être le doute et tu n'es que raison
Tu es le grand soleil qui me monte à la tête
Quand je suis sûr de moi.

The phoenix   [1951]

I LOVE YOU

I love you for all the women I have not known
I love you for all the times I did not live
For the smell of the open air and the smell of warm bread
For the snow that melts for the first flowers
For the pure animals man does not frighten
I love you for the sake of loving
I love you for all the women I do not love

Only you reflect me I scarcely see myself
Without you I see only an empty space
Between former days and today
There were all the dead I crossed over on the straw
I couldn't pierce the wall of my mirror
I had to learn life word by word
How we forget

I love you for your wisdom that is not mine
For well-being
I love you against all that is only illusion
For this immortal heart I do not detain
You think you are doubt and you are only reason
You are the great sun that goes to my head
When I am sure of myself.

LE CHÂTEAU DES PAUVRES (fragment)

. . . . .

Le long effort des hommes vers leur cohésion
Cette chaîne qui sort de la géhenne ancienne
Est soudée à l'or pur au feu de la franchise
Elle respire elle voit clair et ses maillons
Sont tous des yeux ouverts que l'espoir égalise

La vérité fait notre joie écoute-moi
Je n'ai plus rien à te cacher tu dois me voir
Tel que je suis plus faible et plus fort que les autres
Plus fort tenant ta main plus faible pour les autres
Mais j'avoue et c'est là la raison de me croire

J'avoue je viens de loin et j'en reste éprouvé
Il y a des moments où je renonce à tout
Sans raisons simplement parce que la fatigue
M'entraîne jusqu'au fond des brumes du passé
Et mon soleil se cache et mon ombre s'étend

Vois-tu je ne suis pas tout à fait innocent
Et malgré moi malgré colères et refus
Je représente un monde accablant corrompu
L'eau de mes jours n'a pas toujours été changée
Je n'ai pas toujours pu me soustraire à la vase

Mes mains et ma pensée ont été obligées
Trop souvent de se refermer sur le hasard
Je me suis trop souvent laissé aller et vivre
Comme un miroir éteint faute de recevoir
Suffisamment d'images et de passions
Pour accroître le poids de ma réflexion

Castle of the poor [1952-1953]

CASTLE OF THE POOR

. . . .

The long effort of men to come together
A chain that leads out of ancient Gehenna
Soldered to pure gold in the fire of freedom
Breathes sees clearly and its links
Are all open eyes made equal by hope

Truth makes our joy so listen
I have nothing more to hide you must see me
As I am weaker and stronger than the others
Stronger holding your hand weaker for theirs
I admit that is the reason to believe me

I confess I come from afar I have been tried
There are times when I give up
Without reason just because weariness
Leads me to the bottom of past foggy days
My sun hides my shadow grows long

Know that I am not wholly innocent
Inspite of myself my anger and refusals
I represent a corrupt oppressive world
The water of my days has not been replaced
I could not always pull out of the mire

My hands and thoughts too often obliged
To grasp at chance too often I let myself go living
Like a dark mirror for lack of receiving
Enough images and strong feelings
To increase the depth of my reflection

. . . .

Le château des pauvres [1952-1953]

Il me fallait rêver sans ordre sans logique
Sans savoir sans mémoire pour ne pas vieillir
Mais ce que j'ai souffert de ne pouvoir déduire
L'avenir de mon coeur fugitif dis-le toi
Toi qui sais comment j'ai tenté de m'associer

À l'espoir harmonieux d'un bonheur assuré
. . . .

Castle of the poor [1952-1953]

I had to dream without order or logic
Without knowledge or memory to keep from growing old
How I have suffered unable to deduce
The future of my fugitive heart tell me so
You who know how hard I tried to be part

Of the common hope for certain happiness

. . . .

V

Declarations, Essays & Lectures

1925 - 1952

La poésie doit être faite par tous, non par un.
(Poetry should be made by all, not by one alone)

Lautréamont

The Surrealist experiment began with an impelling desire to overcome the complacency of those who were unprepared for World War I, and those who were too willing to compromise with the invaders. Almost an entire generation of young Frenchmen lost their lives in that war. Civil war in Spain (1936-1939) between the Republicans and the Nationalists led by Francisco Franco, and the rise of independence movements in other countries, increased the artists' desire to contribute to the consciousness-raising that might help people to become "fully human" in a democratic world.

The Declaration of 1925 articulates the Surrealists' changing goals. At the International EXPO in Paris on October 2, 1937, Eluard defends the practical use of poetry, in the tradition of bards and troubadours, to tell the history and to raise the people's consciousness of the human condition ("The Future of Poetry").

"Involuntary poetry and intentional poetry" (1942) defends the idea that poetry can be heard in the street, it is made by all of us, not by a solitary poet; for we are all poets, when we choose our words to convey personal, political and social concerns ("The poetry of circumstance," 1952).

On the use of images in this endeavor, two essays recall Picasso's great influence as an artist and as a friend.

Declaration of January 27, 1925[1]

In regard to a false interpretation of our attempt, stupidly broadcast to the public, we must declare the following to all the idiotic contemporary literary, dramatic, philosophical, exegetic, even theological criticism:

1. We have nothing to do with literature; but we are very capable, when necessary, to use it like everyone else.

2. *Surrealism* is not a new or easier means of expression, not even a metaphysics of poetry. It is a means of total liberation of the mind.

3. We are firmly resolved to make a Revolution.

4. We have joined the word *surrealism* to the word *revolution* solely to show the disinterested, detached, even totally desperate character of that revolution.

5. We do not intend to change people's morality, rather we intend to show the fragility of their thinking, and on what shifting terrain, what hollow ground, they have placed their trembling houses.

6. We challenge Society with this solemn warning: Let people pay attention to their faulty directions, to every error of their minds; we shall not miss our mark.

7. Society will find us at every turn of its thought.

8. We are specialists of Revolt. There is no means of action we are not capable of using, if necessary.

9. We speak especially to the western world: *surrealism* exists

— But what is this new *ism* that attaches itself to us?

—*Surrealism* is not a poetic form. It is the outcry of the spirit that looks in on itself and is desperately determined to crush its shackles, if need be with material hammers!

From the bureau of surrealist research: 15, rue de Grenelle

(signed by) Louis Aragon, Antonin Artaud, Jacques Baron, Joe Bosquet, J.-A. Boiffard, André Breton, Jean Carrive, René Crevel, Robert Desnos, Paul Eluard, Max Ernst, T. Fraenkel, Francis Gérard, Michel Leiris, Georges Limbour, Mathias Lubeck, Georges Malkine, André Masson, Max Morise, Pierre Naville, Marcel Noll, Benjamin Péret, Raymond Queneau, Philippe Soupault, Dédé Sunbeam, Roland Tual.

---

[1] Published in the first issue of *La Révolution Surréaliste*, 1925. Signed by the Surrealist writers and painters.

The future of poetry[1] [1937]

I

Bread is more useful than poetry. But love in the complete, most human sense of the word, passionate love, is not more useful than poetry.

II

The poet is much more the one who inspires, than one who is inspired.

III

Observers and faithful mirrors. It is not necessarily those who are in love who have written the best love poems, but when it is, they did not make their beloved responsible for them. However, the reflection of all these words is based on their indelible existence. They have to support this reflection and remain ever ready to reflect and to see, the eternal virtue. Seeing is receiving, reflecting is allowing others to see.

IV

The poet's role will be reduced to that of organizing ideas, objects, feelings, action.

V

It is said that beginning with words and their relationships, to study the world scientifically is not only our right but our duty. It should be added that this duty is the same as living, not in the manner of those who carry their death within themselves, who are already walls or empty shells, but by becoming one with the universe in motion, evolving.

VI

We need few words to express what is essential; we need all the words to make it real.

VII

The poet sees to the extent that he *reveals* himself. And *visa versa,* one day every person will demonstrate what the poet has seen. That will be the end of the imaginary.

VIII

Seeing means understanding, judging, deforming, comparing, forgetting or forgetting oneself, being or disappearing.

IX

Poetry will become flesh and blood only when it is reciprocal. This reciprocity is entirely a function of the equality of happiness among men. Such shared happiness would bring this state of being to heights we can only imagine. That good fortune is not impossible.

X

Sign what you approve of.

XI

There are great expanses in the night. Reasoning has the sole merit of making use of them. In its better moments, it avoids them. Poetry dissipates them.. This is the art of casting light upon obscurity.

XII

This is not a play on words: everything is relative to everything else, everything finds its echo, its reason, its resemblance, its opposition, its becoming, everywhere. This process of becoming is infinite.

---

[1]These twelve principles served to relate readings at a poetic séance of the International Exposition of Paris, October 2, 1937. Published in *Poésie et Vérité* (1942).

Involuntary poetry and intentional poetry [1942]

Personal poetry has had its time of relative tricks and contingent contortions. Let us once again take up the indestructible thread of impersonal poetry.

Comte de Lautréamont

. . . .

What a pity that poetry should have a special name and that poets should form a special class! It is nothing unusual, it is a natural expression of the human mind. Isn't everyone a poet and a thinker, at every moment? There are times when alphabets and account books seem poetic....A true letter is poetic.

Novalis

. . . .

I loved sentimental paintings, images over doorways, decors, paintings of circus performers, signs, popular illuminations; literature gone out of style, Church Latin, erotic books without writing, the novels of our grandparents, fairy tales, little children's books, old operas, silly refrains, naïve rhythms.

Arthur Rimbaud

. . . .

True poets never believed poetry to be theirs alone. On human lips, speech has never dried up; words, songs, cries go on without end, cross each other, bump into each other, mingle....Words tell of the world and of people, what we see and feel...the past and the future of an age, the moment, premeditated or involuntary acts, the fear of and desire for what does not exist and what may be. Words....participate in the elaboration of Truth....

Men have devoured a dictionary; what they name exists. What cannot be named, the finality of everything, begins only at the frontiers of unthinkable death....Language is common to all and it is not the differences between languages...that risk compromising human unity, but the interdiction of the absolute freedom of language. Those who maintain that there are a thousand ways of seeing...a thousand ways of telling of one's love and joy and pain...are taken for madmen. Useless, crazy and accursed are those who disclose, reproduce, interpret the humble voice that complains or sings in the crowd, unaware that it is sublime.

Alas, personal poetry has not yet run its course. At least we have understood that nothing has been able to break the thin thread of impersonal poetry. Without doubting for a moment that truth will triumph, we have heard that so many things can be "just a poem." Poets of good faith have returned this ironic, perjorative expression to its literal meaning. They use objective elements, everything that lies beneath the apparent impermeability of contemporary life, in the most innocent acts of creation.

"A whole poem" is no longer just a deformed object or the eccentricity of a breathless, elegant woman; rather [it is] what the poet is inspired to simulate, reproduce or invent, if he believes that out of the world he is given will be born the universe of his dreams. There is nothing rare or divine in this ordinary endeavor.[1]

The poet, on the lookout for obscure events of the world, will delight us with the purest language of the man in the street and the sage, of woman, of the child and of the insane....Let us listen to them, without reflecting, and respond; then we will be heard. Otherwise, we are only broken mirrors, anxious to improve appearances, poeticizing, withdrawing our first, elementary view of things into a private space and time.

If we wished, nothing would be impossible for us. The most deprived, like the richest, using his hands and eyes with confidence, has the capacity to regain an invaluable treasure: his dream and the reality that reason or ill will cannot destroy.

Involuntary poetry, however banal, imperfect and crude as it may seem, is made of the relationships between human lives and the world, between dreams and love, between love and necessity. It affects our emotions, it returns the lightness of fire to our blood. Everyone is the brother of Prometheus.[2] *Poets do not have a separate intelligence; we are moral beings and we are part of the crowd.*

---

[1] *"Tout un poème", ce n'est plus seulement un objet biscornu ou l'excentricité d'une élégante à bout de souffle, mais ce qu'il est donné au poète de simuler, de reproduire, d'inventer, s'il croit que du monde qui lui est imposé naîtra l'univers qu'il rêve.* (Italics this page are the Editor's.)

[2] Prometheus (Gr., "forethought"). In Greek mythology, son of Titan and brother of Atlas, made man out of clay, then stole fire from the gods to animate his creations. As punishment, Zeus chained him to Mount Caucasus, where an eagle preyed on his liver by day; it was renewed at night. Eventually he was rescued by Hercules.

Picasso good master of liberty[1]   [1948]

1

Picasso, I see you here, I call your name.

I have known your face for a long time, I see it quickly and I see it slowly. A face of my family, a big family of steadfast friends, friends of the day and the night, all quite good-looking, all very different. Good people...ready to extend a paw as a bear reaches for honey. But it is you, Picasso, they embrace first of all, for they are obliged to you for giving order to their behavior. You make them humble or proud, in the sphere of wounds or bruises where they are only men among men.

You show them they can get by with a happy utopia and the childlike dream of an endless vacation, but you also show them how to understand and see everything. You give them the daily courage to refuse to be bound by mortal appearances.

One fine day, they will laugh at having been thirsty and hungry...at having been so often nourished on themselves.

Picasso, your face reflects their cares and pains, and so do the faces of the women they love.

2

You give yourself totally to your work, in youth as in age, you work to uncover your eyes, to lay bare what they see, in all you create. So are you armed against death, against the body's complaints, against neglect and repentance.

3

Let people say you are *a painter*...and *a man*....Let them say you have labored. In the sacred places of mediated laziness, your work, one day, will be honored. Your work has the weight of all useful work.

4

I write for your friends, who are legion. I write for everyone.

---

[1] "Picasso bon maître de la liberté" accompanies photos by Michel Sima of Picasso at work, in *Picasso à Antibes*, Paris: E. Drouin, 1948.

But I write beside a bottomless chasm from which work alone can keep me. I write with bricks and iron scaffolding, a wheelbarrow, a burning flame, the energy of despair. I write to you from a bed half caved in by death.[1]

For you, life is always conquered. I see you building your house, lighting your fire, cutting bread, loving a woman, making children, serving your brothers—refusing to play the infamous game where men are rivals.

5

You refuse to enter the idiot refuge. You go on, still following the exhausting contour of vagabond forms, the cord of early births...the crown of the human sea, the body, the heart and mind. The human body imposed itself on you with its warm hearth, its wings....

You go into the street with confidence....we are strengthened by the knowledge that others are there, that we are many and faithful only outside ourselves, outside prisons....

Oh my brother, my opposite, the world divides infinitely, but gathers itself together as well.

6

At this point I could call up your loves. I have the right to do so, for I rest my hand on your shoulder, to support myself....You would sustain thousands like me, you are the rock from which hopeful men throw themselves into the unknown with all their senses, in the innocence that makes them right—thousands of captive men and women, suddenly made free by a word, a gesture, a look, by eyes, a mouth, a body that open all the doors. Daylight reveals all the treacherous nets of the world, the horizon clouds over and roads disappear into nowhere. Over the bare land the sun leads us on.

Calling up your present loves—and my lost loves—it is good to speak of what we love and have loved. You are happy and I have been so.... Look at me: I am almost blind yet I love the light. Look, since you know how to give definitive form to what passes by and to perpetuate the image that lies on our table; for seeing and understanding go together.

---

[1]Eluard was still grieving for the loss of his beloved Nusch, who died in 1946.

The forms you create, a crowd of portraits, sensitive and confident, mirrors of truth, have no right to know the night.

My gentle friend, the whole ocean is before us, complete. We touch it yet don't see it. You persuade me that I can see the one I loved, even without touching her. You know the whole space between...the varied objects of our dreams and desires, between waking and sleeping, the hand and the cloud, between the flesh and its double.

[You are] the science of proportions, the knowledge of the possible, balance in the conquest of the real; like the rainbow you are friend of man and beast, enamoured of what is worth loving. You recognize in woman the variable image of woman, the one who always negates drought and forgetting; you prepare her bed, you laugh with pleasure.

It would be black misery to see only oneself, to stop on the threshold of the world...to greet oneself as a mortal and then to step backwards.

You love in solidarity, to prove life, loving with good logic. Generous, you let others see.

7

Having had so much to see beyond your hand, you take care to show and to astonish. Having had so much to see in the course taken by your hand, you give confidence to the hands of others.

You know that many of us, because of our fatigue, do not see, much less reproduce the world. Walking alone is a punishment; we don't go far....When we cry out from our prison...no one hears us, no one even imagines us, we are not even imagined. Yet you do not hold it against us....For you know that the least fissure projects us out into the day, you know that it takes only a little space of springtime to free every being on earth, to open our hands, to increase our good will and force the future. You know the highest walls, but you are not in their shadow. Do you suffer less for that?

Haven't you seen....the three serious wrinkles on your face, one between the eyebrows, and two, best defined, from the transverse of the nose to the angle of the chin, three inscriptions that your disconcerting pupils have carved there on the blackboard. The human countenance frolics. But its evolutions won't let it lose hold of its skeleton, or marry the star or the vanilla bean. At most, the wild monkey orchid or a milestone....

Your eyes nourish your hand; perhaps they never close. And your hand is heavy with a germinating seed. Your eyes are the forge, your hand is the mother. Light on one side, time on the other—it's like an axe that divides the world in two, that fells not the tree, but the forest, not the diamond desert, but the whole living anthill....In the window across the way, a woman holds her newborn child in her arms. Like you, she has with her the other half of the world.

8

You don't leave shadows to their fate, you don't wish to limit life— the life of your eyes and of your hands.

Your flag flies against the wind. You go forward fighting. You know your battle, you don't know fatigue. You know everything by heart.

Still, you are accessible, respectful and kind, good and charming. Until the shadow rolls out from deep eyes, believing they have rights over you, my proud savage, my big brother, up to the moment you feel responsible for your brothers, for their cause. The future depends on it. Their cause is just—and you are just.

9

Your work is the full pitcher of water that a girl carries on her head. She is focusing hard on her center of gravity. She retains and develops her movements, her stillness, lengthens her neck, improves her ankles, attaches her breasts a little higher.

In your clearest work the tempest and the shivering wheat are exalted.

We have the world behind and in front of us. Accomplished work is work still to be done, for in the time it takes to turn around, that work has changed. Everything is to be reinvented incessantly, seen again; working becomes a pleasure.

Your desire to know leads you beyond yourself, you never repeat yourself. In this monotonous world you are like a growing child, each day losing a little of yesterday's heart, every day on an unknown path. My dear child, what man will you become? For you surpass the eternal promises of the masters, and their slavish memories are heard crying out, the old vexations are dying.

10

Are we model friends? Yes, as all men must become friends.

Tomorrow, in the well kept place of our hearts, there will be a crowd united, intelligent, happy— victorious.

Picasso Drawings[1] [1952]

When the long film of Picasso's art plays in my memory, I am always struck with admiration for the enthusiasm, the work, the incessant motion of a man whose message I am sure will remain "the best testimony we can give to our dignity."

Picasso's enthusiasm never slows down. That is his strength and his secret. Every step forward opens up a new horizon for him. The past does not hold him; the world opens to him, a world where everything is still to be done and not to be repeated, a world where he is born to himself every day.

It matters little to him to be held up to ridicule, scorned or hated...disavowed by people. He is there to serve the best in them. He knows his enthusiasm is useful, indispensable. It is up to the crowd to understand that there is no enthusiasm without wisdom, nor wisdom without generosity. Picasso's generosity is expressed by work, a work equal to a life that strives to see everything, to project on the screen of man's history everything he can understand, accept, represent or transfigure....There is only one way to draw, it is the motion of the mind and of the hand....

It is said that the greatest painters have painted with their blood. That...image draws its value from the fact that humans have nothing more precious to give. Blood is above all faith in life, its continuity, the perpetuity of human warmth...deep thought and imagination that struggle against death, the will as reasonable as it is capricious....Picasso [is] a man in constant metamorphosis. His eyes, his hands are never anchored. His memory, immense and persistent, has overwhelmed accepted order and convention, reinforcing values established by his peers. Following the drawings Picasso signs Ruiz (his father's name), drawings reminiscent of Toulouse-Lautrec, so severe and pure, the Blue Period surges forth [with its] prodigious nocturnal light. As black plastic throws a new light on Cezanne, we witness the most astonishing resolution of the real: Cubism. Surely Picasso has heard the crystal glass of Ingres ring better than anyone, but into it he poured an inebriating wine. Certainly the Greeks transmitted...their mythological credo, but he has crossed it with modern wisdom and imagination that does not revere the

---

[1] Eluard wrote "Picasso dessins" to accompany sixteen of Picasso's drawings made from 1942-1946 (Braun, la Collection Plastique, 1952).

gods. His astonishing minotaurs, his sirens, his centaurs and fauns live on this earth with a life at once animal and human....

Recently Picasso has become interested in the Middle Ages, by way of romanticism. Immediately another light bathed this past, for us theatrical and somewhat grotesque. The Middle Ages no longer had one way of seeing. Picasso made it *voyant*, giving it the power to join its naïveté, even its brutality, with our contradictory desire for innocence and knowledge.

That is how Picasso is linked to continuing human progress. While we cannot see the influences and origins, he is more completely animated by his own time or he is utopian. From his own time, we have the bathers...harlequins...portraits like bizarre clocks where one eye marks the minutes, the other the hours, where lines come apart, tie together and break like threads of glass, those *natures mortes* where a pipe and a bottle are framed by a newspaper...from his time come all the landscapes bound by morning fogs or the setting sun...*Guernica* or the *Massacres of Korea.* But from tomorrow comes the Dove, and all the writing of dreams while he is awake, those eternal sculptures that tell of human hope, always more beautiful than the present....

Picasso's drawing reestablishes the truth of things, for out of an appearance that is infinitely variable, from billions of instants, he derives a constant, he eternalizes the totality of images, finds the sum of his experiences.

In Picasso's work the search for the definitive formula results in spontaneity and the need for immediate revelation. When Picasso applies himself, it is not to reproduce but to produce. He wants to convince instantly by a single stroke, a single word that shouts the evidence....

And we recognize, across the gravitations and falls of his universe, the reason for our outlook. Mystery is torn apart in suffering, in grief, in anger and in the passion of living. Like love born of worry and *ennui*, clarity and truth often surge up out of days of despair, of furor and rebellion. Picasso has always taken the world seriously and has risked himself wholly, as much when painting a landscape, a still-life or a portrait as when he expresses his social, national and international convictions. What realism...too often lacks is the *feeling* for what is real. We support it with our hearts and our blood coursing, the waves of our hands, the torrent of our eyes. One must have a passion for what is real, and live it. We do not obey objectivity nor do we believe the world that determines us to be immutable...we have confidence in ourselves who come from that world and have assimilated and interpreted its life forces....

In 1936, Picasso depicted the tragedy of an entire people. There are few angry paintings as searing as *Guernica*....the faces of his studies for *Guernica* express supreme suffering...they do not accept, they sweat with anger, spit out the black air of man's shame and crime, as he destroys his fellow man....

"History and poetry can be one," wrote Lope de Vega. Even when men tear each other apart, they make history together. The poet, the painter as well, is with them. But his duty and power choose reality; he wants it to be profound and moral. And if evil itself can lead to something beautiful in his art, beauty can only lead to what is good. The perfections of his Blue Period, the desperate realism of Cubism, his genius for beauty give Picasso an ever growing awareness, expanding his feeling for the indispensible human presence.

The Poetry of circumstance [1] [1952] (excerpts)

If there is one subject which disturbs the poets of our time, surely it is that of circumstantial poetry. They find it disheartening and repugnant. Too many rhymesters, too many prosaic songwriters have tried it; and poetry that endures, man's constant support, at times appears threatened by it. We do not wish to neglect this menace, nor to ignore the imitations, the derision of poetry, nor underestimate its danger. We owe it to ourselves to defend the true poetry of circumstance.

I should have liked to call these reflections: "From circumstantial poetry to eternal poetry," but I gave in to the appeal of a simple title that names this poetry without disclosing its resonance. For there are not two kinds of poetry, and the adjectives we apply to it—lyrical, epic, heroic, didactic, dramatic, rhythmic, free or light—do not keep us from hearing, first of all, the word "poetry", that is, "song". It is language that sings....

In Greece I was presented as a poet to illiterate peasants and they all responded: "Oh, yes! A singer!" Since ancient times, poetry is the language that sings; I think that will never change. "They can take away my life," Aragon says in the preface to *Les yeux d'Elsa;* "but they will never silence my song."

Language that sings is language bearing hope, even when it is desperate, because it is the carrier of profound intelligence, reason founded on instinct...on the need to live, on the love of life, on truth. When a poet calls on death...he does it out of spite. If he invents a god, the world is responsible. And when he loses his reason at the doors of madness to be swallowed up by a huge pile of ruins, let's see how courageous he has been and see his initial zest for life. We must ask if he struggled before being undone by the world....I think this was the way of the men of the Middle Ages and François Villon, the men of the Commune[2] and Arthur Rimbaud[3]...In human history, material deprivation

---

[1] A lecture at the Salle des Sociétés Savantes, January 17, 1952; published in *La Nouvelle Critique*, April 1952, 32-44.

[2] In 1871 the proletarian insurgents of the Commune refused to accept the agreements of the French government with the Prussian generals who had defeated the French armies. French troops executed 15,000 insurgents.

[3] Arthur Rimbaud, who greatly influenced the symbolist poets, abandoned poetry and France in 1873 at the age of 19, to seek his fortune in Africa.

has too often brought with it moral deprivation...many others resisted and yet were vanquished. Whitman...Shelley, Nerval...Apollinaire... Maiakovski, Lorca and Robert Desnos, heroes or victims, all yearned for a greater light.[1] They incarnate man...subjugated and in revolt, enslaved while dreaming of liberty....

Other poets show a stronger, more serene countenance...a little like saints, they have put on a mask of wisdom: Homer, Shakespeare, Dante, Goethe. They have reigned and their voice is...as impersonal as that of the popular, anonymous, fearless poets who sing in public places....When they say "I" they speak for the people of their time. They are the conscience of their time, they bear witness to the great trial of history....

[These were] great voices, but do we not respond more to those who represent our precarious condition, who express our hopes and desires...as well as our pain, our common human measure? Like Villon among the brigands, Whitman caring for the wounded, Pushkin fallen in a duel over his wife's honor, Max Jacob dying because he was Jewish.... Injustice inflames our passion for justice. Too much energy has been wasted, too much intelligence subservient to evil.... their action, words and example live on through us....We know the circumstances of their lives.

The dictionary calls circumstance "a common place" (*lieu commun*), including what relates to the person...his methods, his motives...and his time. Criticism of men and their works must consider all the conditions....It will judge how a man was changed by the circumstances, and to what degree they raised him up or degraded him. A moral person identifies not only with those who are close to him, but with those he doesn't know, the events that affect them and that they provoke. So the poet burns to reproduce life.

The world, says Goethe, is so vast, and life offers such a diverse spectacle that subjects for poetry will never be lacking. But this is always circumstantial poetry; reality must furnish the occasion and the material. A particular case becomes general and poetic...My poems are all poems of circumstance.

---

[1] Shelley died at 30 from drowning; Nerval and Maiakovski committed suicide; Apollinaire, wounded in World War I, died in 1918 from Spanish influenza; Federico Garcia-Lorca was shot by the Spanish militia; Desnos died after the Allied troops liberated the Jews at Auschwitz.

We can't say that reality lacks poetic interest; a poet proves himself precisely when his mind can discover an interesting side to a banal subject. Reality provides the motive, the point of departure, the nugget...the poet's business is to turn it into a beautiful, animated whole....Through his sensitivity and understanding the poet is like a set of scales for weighing everything about human life and universal life....Obscure circumstances are illuminated by the poet's pen, reflected in a mirror that elucidates them, visible for all of us....

Every poem is one of circumstance. But whether we understand this word in its broadest sense or in its narrow sense, this poem...will not attain its goal unless it escapes mediocrity....The ideal reader is skeptical; he knows that being conscious in the pursuit of evil ways is sometimes less dangerous than being unconscious in good acts; he is on guard against hypocrisy; he knows to what point...we can be misled by taking the easy way out, or by "letting go."

True poetry must express the real world, our interior world and the world transformed that we dream of—that truth within ourselves if our eyes are truly open....the poet will never be able to give back to the world more than abstraction and confusion, formless dreams and absurd beliefs if he has not carried his own weight in the world or the weight of the world, himself....It is easy to give in to one's lassitude, to one's grief, easier to commit suicide than to live, especially with responsiblity.

To find the whole of what is out there, one must have the courage to add up objects and feelings, one's love and hate, colors and forms, epochs and climates, those thousands of ways that bring William Blake to say that "men are equal by their differences." The poet will ally his sensitivity, his judgment, his imagination to this real world that he must...transform. He will do it with passion, and if he wholly commits himself, he will emerge a winner over the inevitable struggles between good and evil, youth and decadence, armed hate and love that regenerates itself.

It is a question of rising with immemorial and future crowds above the fetid mud of the oppression of man by man, of the poet by the philistine, of the martyr by the assassin. Human thought must find a healthy character once again, restore its unity and the joy of living, [and find again] that philosophical stone.

We know that poetic genius exists only to the degree the poet does not distort the truth. And not lying today means taking action. May poetry be a means of action, of moving forward, for it sings out from all windows and on all the horizons, it sings the evidence and the example contradicting the lie....Just as the fruits and flowers are the circumstances of spring, so revolution can be the circumstance for a people's happiness....The revolutionary poem must find its inspiration in clear feelings founded on the necessity of living and reproducing life, on a well defined, logical desire for justice. However, because this feeling is founded on human association, it must have a poetic content as dense as the feeling of love, another expression of the struggle for life.

We must take hold of reality, control it. This reality...does not wear a mask...it can be called idiocy, misery, sickness, war. Above all the poet must not give in to that singular melancholy that would associate him with those Lautréamont called "the great soft Heads." Nor must he consider that the paths of poetry are narrow and its forms unchangeable. Every brave poet must open a broad path...to human exaltation. For that all forms are good....There are no more sacred forms than there are sacred, profane or vulgar subjects or words....

Here then is today's fairytale. Human work and intelligence replace the fairy ring, creative instrument of images. We have known the legend of terrestrial paradise. Only a curse came of it....Many of us need only a little more conscience, an awareness of human possibilities and of the possibilities of poetry....So that a poem may move from the particular to the general and take on a valuable, universal meaning, circumstance must agree with the poet's simplest desires, with his heart, mind and reason. If it doesn't...it is lost in the moment...it lasts only the length of time it took to be sung....

While writing a poem on miners on strike or for the liberation of Henri Martin,[1] our poets are conscious of singing of a circumstance tied to the future, by which man takes a step towards life. I will take a personal example, that of my poem "Liberté." I wrote this poem during the summer of 1941. While composing the first stanzas:

> *Sur mes cahiers d'écolier*
> *Sur mon pupitre et les arbres*
> *Sur le sable sur la neige*
> *J'écris ton nom*

---

[1] Henri Martin was imprisoned for encouraging Frenchmen to refuse to participate in the war in French Indo-China (Vietnam) during the years following World War II. They were replaced by U.S. forces until 1975.

I intended to reveal, at the end, the name of the woman I loved, for whom this poem was destined. I soon realized that the only word I had in mind was the word "liberty:"

> *Et par le pouvoir d'un mot*
> *Je recommence ma vie*
> *Je suis né pour te connaître*
> *Pour te nommer*
> *Liberté.*[1]

So the woman I loved embodied a desire greater than herself. I fused her with my highest hope, and this word liberty throughout my poem was only to eternalize the very ordinary desire of freeing ourselves from the occupiers. This indispensable idea of liberty is an unlimited ideal...each step we take must be a liberation....The idea of liberation is...the very idea of progress, the continual progress against fatality, towards that dream of total freedom....

Memory fades but conscience subsists....True circumstantial poetry must come from the poet with the precision of a mirror as faithful as the flower nurtured by spring, like the joy of building for living....

French poetry emerged considerably improved from the trials France experienced during the war of occupation....because the horizon broadened and we no longer believed any subject to be unsuitable. It found again...patriotic feeling came closer to the unfortunate, to lead the war against oppression and war; it found a collective voice.

This voice must prevail....for the menace bears down on us once again. The song in defense of peace rises everywhere .... peace represented by the symbol of the dove....defended by its pure white, colored by a fire lit by Prometheus that blinds the birds of prey. Poets know that peace is the order of the day...the only possible future. Neither the birds nor our hearts will stop singing.

---

[1] In my schoolboy's notebook/On my desk and the trees/On the sand on the snow/I write your name....And by the power of a word/I begin my life again/I am born to know you/to name you/Liberty.

BIBLIOGRAPHY

Primary works by Paul Eluard

Oeuvres Complètes, Vols. I & II. Lucien Scheler & Marcelle Dumas, eds. Paris: Gallimard, Bibliothèque de la Pléiade, 1968.

A toute épreuve. Wood engravings by Joan Miro. Geneva: George Cramer, 1958. NY: Braziller. Introduction by Anne Hyde Greet, 1984.

Anthologie des écrits sur l'art. I. *Les frères voyants*, 1952. II. *Morale*, 1953. III. *La passion de peindre*, 1954. Paris: Editions Cercle d'art.

Lettres à Gala, 1924-1948. Editions Pierre Dreffus. Préface de Jean-Claude Carrière. Paris: Gallimard, 1984.

Paul Eluard. Le poète et son ombre: Proses 1920-1952. R.D.Valette, ed. Paris: Seghers, 1967.

"Trois conférences inédites de Paul Eluard", "L'Amour en guerre." Lucien Scheler, ed. Paris: *Europe*, Oct. 1982. 145-166.

Uninterrupted Poetry. Lloyd Alexander, ed. and trans. With forewords by L. Aragon, Louis Parrot, Claude Roy. NYC: New Directions, 1975.

Voir. Poèmes, peintures, dessins. Genève: Trois Collines, 1948.

Lectures and Essays by Eluard

"Déclaration du 27 janvier, 1925". *La Révolution Surréaliste*, Jan. 1925.

"Avenir de la poésie." Paris: G.L.M., 1937.

Poésie involontaire et poésie intentionelle. Paris: Eds. *Poésie et vérité*, 1942. Preface to quotations chosen by P. Eluard. Paris: Seghers, 1963.

"Picasso bon maître de la liberté". *Picasso à Antibes*. Paris: E. Drouin, 1948.

"Picasso, dessins." *Picasso, dessins*. Paris: Editions Braun et Cie, 1952.

"La poésie de circonstance". *La Nouvelle Critique*, avril 1952.

Selected Critical Works

Aragon, Louis *"La peinture au défi."* *Les Collages*. Paris: Hermann, 1965. 35-70.

347

Bachelard, Gaston. "Germe et raison dans la poésie de Paul Eluard" in *Le droit de rêver*. Paris: Presses Universitaires de France, 1970. 169-195.

Balakian, Anna. *Surrealism: the road to the absolute*. N.Y: Noonday Press. 1959.

Bergez, Daniel. *Eluard ou le rayonnement de l'être*. Champ Vallon, 1982.

Breton, André. *Entretiens, 1913-1952, avec André Parinaud...* [etc.] Paris: Gallimard, 1952. In 16. 319.

Decaunes, Luc. *Paul Eluard. L'amour, la révolte, le rêve*. Paris: Balland, 1982.

Eluard et ses amis peintres. Paris: Centre Georges Pompidou, 1982.

Gateau, Jean Charles. *Eluard, Picasso et la peinture* (1936-1952). Geneva: Droz , 1983.

— *Paul Eluard et la peinture surréaliste*. Geneva: Droz, 1983.

Hobsbawm, Eric. *The Age of Extremes. A History of the World, 1914-1991*. New York: Pantheon Books, 1994.

Jean, Raymond. *Paul Eluard*. Paris: Seuil, 1968.

Marcenac, Jean. Postface to *Paul Eluard*, L.Parrot, Ed. Paris: Seghers, 1953. 217-262.

Matthews, J.H. *Surrealist Poetry in France*. Syracuse, N.Y.: Syracuse University Press. 1969.

Nadeau, Maurice. *The History of Surrealism*. Translated from the French by Richard Howard. New York: MacMillan, 1975.

Parrot, Louis. Préface. *Paul Eluard*. Seghers, 1948. 6-89.

Poulet, Georges. "Eluard" in *Le point de départ*. Paris: Plon, 1964. 128-160.

Read, Herbert, Ed. Introduction to *Surrealism*. With essays by A. Breton, Hugh S. Davies, Paul Eluard, Georges Hugnet. NY: Harcourt, Brace, 1937. 1-91.

Richard, Jean Pierre. "Paul Eluard". *Onze études sur la poésie moderne*. Paris: Seuil, 1964. 104-139.

Rubin, William Stanley. *Dada and Surrealist Art*. N.Y: Harry Abrams, 1968.

Seghers, Pierre. *La Résistance et ses poètes*, I & II. Verviers (Belgium): Marabout, 1978.

Senghor, L. "Paul Eluard, le classique de l'unité retrouvée." *Europe* Jan-April, 1953, 169-74.

Vernier, Richard. *Poésie Ininterrompu et la poétique de Paul Eluard*. Hawthorne, NY and the Hague: Mouton Press, 1971.

René Magritte. Ink drawing for the 1946 edition of *Les nécessités de la vie et les conséquences des rêves*. Coll. Musée Saint Denis.

Surrealism is . . .

. . . an instrument of recognition and thereby an instrument of conquest as well as of defense, which works to bring to light the deep consciousness of man, to reduce the differences existing between men.
P. E., *Dictionnaire abrégé du surréalisme* (1938)
Paul Eluard and André Breton, editors

. . . a way to get to the truth; a means of seeing through rationalist explanations to identify the real motivations for human behavior.

. . . seeing a beautiful woman in a bikini under the wing of a huge bird, under a waterfall, drinking a Pepsi. C. B.

Everything leads us to believe that there is a certain point in our awareness when life and death, the real and the imaginary, past and future, the communicable and the uncommunicable, the high and the low, cease to be perceived as contradictory. The motivation of Surrealist activity is none other than the hope for the resolution of this point.
A. B., *Dictionnaire abrégé du surréalisme* (1938)

Other books from the Oyster River Press

Edged in Light. Poems by Jane Baymore Jordan. Illustrated by Charles Chu. 1993. 1 882291 52 2

Halcyon Time. Poems by Hugh Hennedy. Illus. Charles Chu. 1993. 1 882291 54 9

Intense Experience. Social Psychology through Poetry. 1990. Fred Samuels, Ed. 0 9617481 6 8

Is It Poison Ivy? by Joan Raysor Darlington, author and illustrator. 1993. 1 882291 53 0

A Letter to My Daughter, 1687, by the Marquis of Halifax. (1927-1987). With *Essays from a New England College Town* by Phoebe Taylor. 1992. 0 9617481 4 1

The Mending of the Sky and other Chinese Myths. Retold by Xiao Ming Li. Illus. Shan Ming Wu. 1989. 0 9617481 3 3

Peace in Exile. Poems by David Oates. 1992. 0 9617481 9 2

Cassette of readings from the poems 1 882291 50 6

Thoughts for the Free Life. Lao Tsu to the Present. 2nd ed. 1989. P. Taylor, Ed. Illustrated. 0 9617481 5 X